BELTWAY
BLOOPERS

BELTWAY BLOOPERS

Hilarious Quotes and Anecdotes
from Washington, D.C.

METRO BOOKS
NEW YORK

Acknowledgements

Don Reid and Wiggles 3D would like to acknowledge the efforts of the contributing research team of Judy Hemming, Brett Tiltman, Paul Tuns and Peter Nesbitt for making this book a rich collection of political gems.

Don't Quote Me is a registered trademark of Wiggles 3D Incorporated and is used with permission. Don't Quote Me celebrates great quotations and trivia in a series of board games, puzzles, on-line resources and radio, mobile and newspaper syndication services.

www.dontquoteme.com

Metro Books
122 Fifth Ave.
New York, NY 10011

ISBN-13: 978-1-4351-0619-2
ISBN-10: 1-4351-0619-9

Printed and bound in the United States of America

10 9 8 7 6 5 4 3 2 1

The quotations in this book have been drawn from many sources. While every effort has been made to verify the quotes and sources, the publishers cannot guarantee their perfect accuracy.

★ ★ ★

"Oh, Lord. I didn't mean to say anything quotable."

—Defense Secretary Donald Rumsfeld in a Sept. 7, 2001 meeting with the editorial board of the Associated Press

★ ★ ★

Contents

Welcome to *Beltway Bloopers*

Beltway Bloopers celebrates the world's greatest renewable resource—the quotation. Politicians are often measured by the way they can turn a phrase and answer tough questions. Armed with words, the well-equipped political warrior can galvanize a campaign by giving voice to a clear vision of leadership and telling the public what sets them apart from the other candidates.

However, *Beltway Bloopers* illuminates another side of politics where words are not always the political candidate's ally.

The campaign trail is an openly hostile environment and the debates are battlefields. The slightest misstep reveals perceived weakness and could become a feature on the evening news. These gaffes take many forms—verbal jousting that goes bad, misguided policy or revealing doublespeak. The politician's reputation is further tested by barbs from pundits, attacks by other politicians or even dulled by their own family and friends. *Beltway Bloopers* captures the best of these unintentional slip-ups, the funniest of mess-ups, and the truly wrong!

The free world is led by the speakers on these pages. We can only hope...

> — **Don Reid**
> **Creator of Don't Quote Me ®**

Chapter One

★ ★ ★

ON THE CAMPAIGN TRAIL

VOTERS: X MARKS
THE SPOT

"If pigs could vote, the man with the slop bucket would be elected swineherd every time, no matter how much slaughtering he did on the side."
— U.S writer Orson Scott Card in *Saints* (2001)

"It's no exaggeration to say that the undecideds could go either way."
— Vice President George H.W. Bush before the 1988 election

"George Bush was not elected by a majority of the voters in the United States. He was appointed by God."
— Lt. Gen. William Boykin as undersecretary of defense intelligence in June 2003

"Hell, I never vote for anybody. I always vote against."
— humorist W.C. Fields

"Well, you know, I'm electable if you vote for me."

— Rep. Dennis Kucinich (D-OH, 1997–) in 2004 after a panelist in a debate in Des Moines, Iowa said many Democrats didn't think Kucinich was electable

"What is the primary purpose of a political leader? To build a majority.... If [voters] care about parking lots, then talk about parking lots."

— Rep. Newt Gingrich (R-GA, 1979–99), quoted in John M. Barry's *Ambition and the Power* (1989)

"Vote for the man who promises least; he'll be the least disappointing."

— presidential advisor Bernard M. Baruch

"Voters quickly forget what a man says."

— Richard Nixon, 37th U.S. president

FLASHBACK

Following John F. Kennedy's first Senate race in 1952, the future president was met with suggestions from the press that his father, industrialist Joseph P. Kennedy, had bought his Senate victory. In the wake of this criticism, J.F.K. pretended to read out a telegram at the Gridiron Club in Washington, D.C. The "telegram," which he claimed came from his father, ran: "Dear Jack: Don't buy a single vote more than necessary. I'll be damned if I'll pay for a landslide."

IT'S ALL HOW YOU
LOOK AT IT

That's an Interesting Spin on It...

"We are in a three-way split decision for third place."

> — Sen. Joseph Lieberman (D-CT) describing his fifth-place finish in the 2004 New Hampshire presidential primary for the Democratic party. The final stats were: 1) John Kerry, 39%; 2) Howard Dean, 26%; 3) and 4) John Edwards, 12%, and Wesley Clark, 12%; 5) Lieberman, 9%.

"I am the front-runner… I'm the guy to beat."

> — former Alaska senator Mike Gravel, in 2006, announcing his candidacy for the Democratic presidential nomination. No poll ever ranked Gravel in the top five.

In 2004, CNN's Judy Woodruff interviewed Washington state GOP gubernatorial candidate Dino Rossi, who had won by 42 votes. Woodruff asked, "Are you the winner? Or was this more of a tie?" Rossi responded, "No, a tie is actually when you tie."

FLASHBACK

"I've told you I don't live and die by the polls. Thus, I will refrain from pointing out that we're not doing too bad in those polls."

—George H.W. Bush at a news conference on Nov. 6, 1991

PUTTING THE FUN IN
FUNDRAISING

Candidates have to be creative when it comes to fundraising. Here's how some of them have approached it.

In August 2007, Cindy McCain made an electronic appeal for funds on behalf of her husband, Sen. John McCain. Via an e-mail letter, she asked that supporters give McCain a special gift for his 71st birthday on Aug. 29—two dollars for every year, or a campaign contribution of $142.

Another birthday fundraiser was devised for John Edwards in honor of his 54th birthday on June 10, 2007. The Edwards campaign says that John's favorite pie is his mother's pecan pie. They offered supporters her secret family recipe for $6.10. To boot, campaign aides Joe Trippi and Jonathan Prince created and posted a "homemade" video demonstrating how not to make the pie—the duo ended up burning their attempt.

Here's Dole's Solution

"Some of us are uncomfortable taking honoraria. I am uncomfortable taking campaign contributions. So I compromised: I decided to take both."

— Bob Dole, former chair of the Senate finance committee

BARACK
OBAMA

Sen. Barack Obama (D-IL) announced his candidacy for the 2008 presidency in February 2007. He'd started attracting attention a few years earlier and, in 2005, was named to the Time 100, *Time* magazine's list of the 100 most influential people in the world.

On being the only African-American in the U.S. Senate: "I'm so overexposed, I'm making Paris Hilton look like a recluse."
— **in February 2005**

On being the underdog to win the Democratic candidacy: "I've always been the underdog. When your name is Barack Obama, you are always the underdog. That's a given."
— **Sen. Barack Obama to Jay Leno on** *The Tonight Show* **in October 2007**

"I know that folks were rifling through my kindergarten papers. I'm going to be disclosing them tomorrow. It will show that I experimented with coloring outside the lines. I was pulling on pigtails."
— **in December 2007, in response to Clinton-campaign attacks on Obama's grade school records**

"To prepare for this debate I rode in the bumper cars at the state fair."

— during an Iowa Democratic candidates' debate in August 2007

At a Democratic debate in Las Vegas in January 2008, the participants were asked to name what they saw as their biggest weakness. Barack Obama, who went first, confessed to having a messy desk. Hillary Clinton talked about her impatience about improving life in the United States. John Edwards talked about his strong reaction to seeing people in pain. Later that week, Obama recounted the incident to a crowd of supporters at a town hall meeting in Las Vegas. "Because I'm an ordinary person, I thought that they meant, 'What's your biggest weakness?'" Obama said. "If I had gone last I would have known what the game was. And then I could have said, 'Well, ya know, I like to help old ladies across the street. Sometimes they don't want to be helped. It's terrible.'"

"I am not opposed to all wars. I'm opposed to dumb wars."

— Sen. Barack Obama (D-IL) in an Oct. 2, 2002 speech against the Iraq War

THAT'S DEBATABLE

Political debates allow opponents to square off in public. Here are some of our favorite moments from the debates.

During a January 2004 debate of Democratic presidential candidates, Dennis Kucinich came prepared with visuals. Unfortunately, the debate was broadcast only on radio. The moderator, NPR's Neal Conan, noted to listeners, "Congressman Kucinich is holding up a pie chart, which is not truly effective on radio."

Bill Richardson, a Democratic presidential hopeful, participated in an August 2007 debate. When asked to name something negative and something positive about another candidate, he replied, "Let me just say, I love all of the candidates here. In fact, I think they would all do great in the White House as my vice president."

FLASHBACK

"I will not make age an issue of this campaign. I am not going to exploit, for political purposes, my opponent's youth and inexperience."

— Ronald Reagan, referring to Walter Mondale during a 1984 presidential debate. At the time, Reagan was 73, Mondale was 53.

During a December 2007 Democratic debate, Sen. Barack Obama was asked how he could break from the past while having advisors who had worked for the Clinton administration. Sen. Hillary Clinton laughed and said, "I want to hear that." Obama responded, "Hillary, I look forward to you advising me, as well."

About the Republican presidential debates: "This is a lot like *Law & Order*. It has a huge cast. The series seems to go on forever, and Fred Thompson shows up at the end."

> — 2008 presidential hopeful Mitt Romney, making a dig at Fred Thompson in October 2007. Thompson, a sometime actor, had made several high-profile appearances during the year before officially throwing his hat in the ring for the top job in September.

A New Way to Improve TV Ratings?

The May 2007 Republican debate was held in the Ronald Reagan Library in Simi Valley, California. Reagan's name was mentioned 29 times by both candidates and the moderator. Salena Zito, a columnist for the *Pittsburgh Tribune-Review*, suggested the Reagan Drinking Game. To play the game, viewers would have had to take a drink each time Reagan's name was evoked during the debate.

"Jesus was too smart to ever run for public office."

> — former Arkansas governor Mike Huckabee during a November 2007 GOP debate, when asked whether he thought Jesus would support the death penalty

HILLARY CLINTON:
BRING IT ON!

About the competition for the 2008 Democratic nomination:
"I anticipate it's going to get even hotter, and if you can't stand
the heat get out of the kitchen. And I'm very much at home in
the kitchen."

— Sen. Hillary Clinton at a November 2007 press conference

Maybe *That's* Her Secret...

At the Democratic candidates' debate in Las Vegas in November
2007, CNN's Campbell Brown told Clinton that her opponents say
she avoids taking firm positions on controversial topics. Clinton,
ready to take on all comers, responded, "I am happy to be here
tonight. And this pantsuit, it's asbestos tonight."

An Undiplomatic Remark?

"We've had an administration that doesn't believe in diplomacy.
You know, they have, every so often, Condi Rice go around
the world and show up somewhere and make a speech. And
occasionally, they even send Dick Cheney, and that's hardly
diplomatic in my view..."

— Hillary Clinton in June 2007, during a Democratic debate about U.S.
relations with Iran

RICH MAN,
POOR MAN

While campaigning, politicians often try to show how they're in touch with everyday folk. They don't always succeed.

"This is an impressive crowd—the haves and the have-mores. Some people call you the elites; I call you my base."

> — George W. Bush, joking to the audience at a black-tie fundraiser in October 2000. The $800-a-plate dinner was held in New York City.

During a Democratic presidential nomination debate answering questions posed by regular Americans on YouTube, Sen. Barack Obama (D-IL) said, "Well, we can afford to work for the minimum wage because most folks on this stage have a lot of money. It's the folks... on that screen who deserve—you're doing all right, Chris, compared to, I promise you, the folks who are on that screen." Sen. Christopher Dodd (D-CT) responded, "Not that well, I'll tell you, Barack." As a senator, Dodd earns $165,000 a year and is estimated to be worth $1.5 million to $3.5 million.

"You work three jobs? ... Uniquely American, isn't it? I mean, that is fantastic that you're doing that."

> — President George W. Bush to a divorced mom in Nebraska in 2005

Sen. John Edwards told the BBC in 2004, "I think the key is to see things through the eyes of regular Americans. That's a perspective that people are hungry for." The fortune he amassed from his days as a trial lawyer is estimated to be between $20-70 million; through the mid-2000s he owned four houses and in 2006 he moved into a 29,000 square-foot house.

About the definition of middle class: "Anybody who has to work for a living."

— **Bill Richardson, governor of New Mexico and Democratic presidential hopeful, to Washington's *The Hill* newspaper in July 2007**

In October 2000, while running for president, Vice President Al Gore spoke at a black-tie fundraiser in New York City. Hillary Clinton, then campaigning for a New York senate seat, was in the audience. While on the campaign trail, Gore often drove his points about policy home with real-world examples about "average folk." That night, he won over the elite crowd when he spoke about a "woman who's here tonight, whose husband is about to lose his job. She's struggling to get out of public housing and get a job of her own. Hillary Clinton, I want to fight for you!"

RUNNING FOR
OFFICE

It's on My Resume Under "Special Skills"

"I know one end of a cow from another."

> — former president Bill Clinton, explaining at a state fair in 2006 how he brings political balance when campaigning with his wife, Sen. Hillary Clinton

About his plans to run for governor: "It's the most difficult decision I've ever made in my entire life, except for the one in 1978 when I decided to get a bikini wax."

> — Arnold Schwarzenegger in August 2003 on *The Tonight Show*, announcing his plans to run for governor of California

Pay Attention to Me!

When former senator Mike Gravel announced he was running as Democratic presidential candidate in April 2006, the reaction was a bit muted. After his announcement speech, he addressed the crowd, "I'm sure some of you have some questions." He further prompted reporters by asking, "Who has the first question?" After still no audience response, he asked, "I think there are some press people in the room, aren't there?"

Quite a Shot

"I will not be active in his campaign. I am too busy with golf."

> — Andrew Giuliani in March 2007, on his father's campaign. He's a member of the Harvard golf team.

"It takes a courageous man to decide he's undecided."

> — Fox News' Brit Hume after Sen. Chuck Hagel (R-NE) held a March 2007 press conference to announce he might be prepared to launch a presidential campaign later that year

Why You Should Vote for Me

"We've never had a president named Bob, and I think it's time."

> — Sen. Bob Dole, announcing his presidential candidacy in 1995

Why Run for Office?

"To capitalize on the celebrity nature of the presidential campaign."

> — former senator Mike Gravel, explaining why he was running for the 2008 Democratic presidential nomination

FLASHBACK

"I'll be glad to reply to or dodge your questions, depending on what I think will help our election most."

> — George H.W. Bush to a South Carolina campus while campaigning in 1980

Chapter Two

POLITICAL
MACHINATIONS

A HARSH LOOK AT POLITICS

About politics: "If you can't stand the sight of your own blood, best that you buy a ticket, sit in the stands and watch it from a distance because this is a full-contact sport."

> — **2008 GOP hopeful Mike Huckabee in a December 2007 interview with Larry King on** *Larry King Live*

"In Washington, lying is an art form and a growth industry."

> — **Richard Stengel in an Aug. 31, 1998** *Time* **article,** *Lies My Presidents Told Me.* **Stengel is now managing editor of** *Time* **magazine.**

(On whether he wanted to try for the vice presidency) "You know, I spent all those years in a North Vietnamese prison camp, kept in the dark, fed scraps... why the heck would I want to do that all over again?"

> — **Sen. John McCain (R-AZ) on** *Late Show with David Letterman*, **in February 2007**

"Business is a dog eat dog world, and government is just the opposite."

> — **Michael Bloomberg, New York City mayor, in an appearance on** *The Apprentice* **in October 2004**

NO HOLDS BARRED:
TELL ME WHAT YOU REALLY THINK

Here's a collection of political insults that we love, simply because they are testaments to the power of adjectives.

In December 2003, a conservative group from Iowa aired an attack ad featuring a pair of senior citizens opining, "I think Howard Dean should take his tax-hiking, government-expanding, latte-drinking, sushi-eating, Volvo-driving, *New York Times*-reading, body-piercing, Hollywood-loving, left-wing freak show back to Vermont, where it belongs."

Sen. Kay Bailey Hutchison, speaking at the 1996 GOP national convention, had this to say: "It's time to wake up to President Clinton and his high-taxing, free-spending, promise-breaking, social security-taxing, health care-socializing, drug-coddling, power-grabbing, business-busting, lawsuit-loving, UN-following, FBI-abusing, IRS-increasing, 200-dollar hair-cutting, gas-taxing, over-regulating, bureaucracy-trusting, class-baiting, privacy-violating, values-crushing, truth-dodging, medicare-forsaking, property-rights-taking, job-destroying friends. And that's just in the White House!"

In 2004, filmmaker Michael Moore wrote on his Web site: "I would like to apologize for referring to George W. Bush as a 'deserter.' What I meant to say is that George W. Bush is a deserter, an election thief, a drunk driver, a WMD liar and a functional illiterate. And he poops his pants."

In a 1992 letter, Pat Robertson wrote, "The feminist agenda... is not about equal rights for women. It's about a socialist, anti-family political movement that encourages women to leave their husbands, kill their children, practice witchcraft and become lesbians."

Robert "B1-Bob" Dorman, a long-time California representative, once referred to Sen. Barbara Boxer's liberal supporters as the "coke-snorting, wife-swapping, baby-born-out-of-wedlock radical Hollywood left."

FLASHBACK

Even Abraham Lincoln was not spared. In an 1864 issue, *Harper's Weekly* referred to him as a "filthy story-teller, despot, liar, thief, braggart, buffoon, usurper, monster, old scoundrel, perjurer, swindler, tyrant, field-butcher, land-pirate."

CRINGE-WORTHY COMMENTS

It's too easy to realize that a remark or comment was tasteless or inappropriate after you've said it. These remarks by politicians fall under the heading of "Bad Things to Have Said."

In 2006, then-senator George Allen (R-VA) was seen as a potential candidate for the GOP presidential race in 2008. While on a Virginia tour stop in August, he put his foot in his mouth when referring to an opposing campaign volunteer of Indian descent. He said, "This fellow here, over here with the yellow shirt, macaca, or whatever his name is. He's with my opponent. He's following us around everywhere. And it's just great.... Let's give a welcome to macaca, here. Welcome to America and the real world of Virginia." This remark, captured on video, provoked controversy. "Macaca" is a racial slur used by the French to refer to native Africans. Allen later apologized, saying he didn't know what the word meant. He lost his re-election bid for senator that fall.

FLASHBACK

"This is a great day for France!"

— **President Richard Nixon while attending the funeral of French president Charles de Gaulle in 1970**

"I have just come out of six weeks at a concentration camp held by the Democrat Party of Arkansas in an undisclosed location, making a hostage tape."

> — GOP hopeful Mike Huckabee in October 2006, as the governor of Arkansas, talking on *Imus in the Morning* about his dramatic, 100-pound weight loss

In January 2006, Ray Nagin, mayor of New Orleans, said, "I don't care what people are saying uptown or wherever they are. This city will be chocolate at the end of the day. This city will be a majority African-American city. It's the way God wants it to be." The next day, after negative reactions to this comment, Nagin said he had not intended his comments to be divisive. He said, "How do you make chocolate? You take dark chocolate, you mix it with white milk, and it becomes a delicious drink. That is the chocolate I am talking about."

"Boy, they were big on crematoriums, weren't they?"

> — Vice President George H.W. Bush after a tour of Auschwitz in the fall of 1987

Them Thar's Fightin' Words!

In May 2007, Sen. Sam Brownback gave a speech in Wisconsin. Using a football analogy to talk about the need to focus on families, he said, "This is fundamental blocking and tackling. This is your line in football. If you don't have a line, how many passes can Peyton Manning complete? Greatest quarterback, maybe, in NFL history." This remark drew boos and groans from the audience and the senator realized too late that, in Wisconsin, the Green Bay Packers and quarterback Brett Favre reign supreme. After realizing his faux pas, he said: "That's really bad. That will go down in history. I apologize."

"Bill [Clinton] is every bit as black as Barack—he's probably gone with more black women than Barack."

> — former Atlanta mayor Andrew Young, an African-American, endorsing Hillary Clinton over Barack Obama in December 2007

This Would Make Her Party Cringe

"I'm more comfortable telling people I'm a nudist than saying I'm a Democrat."

> — Idaho resident Terri Capshaw whose home was adjacent to the site of the 61st Annual Northwest Nudists Convention and who raised her family in the nudist lifestyle

HISTORIC
ATTACKS

Political venom certainly isn't new. However, modern attacks usually don't involve comparisons to dessert…

The Gloves Are Off!

"McKinley has no more backbone than a chocolate éclair."

> — Theodore Roosevelt, about President William McKinley. Roosevelt made this remark as a member of McKinley's cabinet in 1898. Roosevelt became president in 1901 after McKinley was assassinated.

With Friends Like These…

"He is vain, irritable, and a bad calculator of the force and probable effect of the motives which govern men."

> — Thomas Jefferson, writing about his friend John Adams in 1787. Adams served as president from 1797–1801. Jefferson served as president from 1801–09.

About Richard Nixon: "He inherited some good instincts from his Quaker forebears, but by diligent hard work, he overcame them."

> — journalist and editor James Reston

ONCE A MOVIE STAR, ALWAYS
A MOVIE STAR

Gov. Arnold Schwarzenegger, a.k.a. Ah-nuld, is a former Mr. Olympia and the star of action movies *Conan the Barbarian*, *The Terminator* and *Total Recall*. In his role as politician, he has a knack for self-promotion and analogies based on the entertainment industry or his movie roles. Here are a few examples.

"I'll be back."

> — at the end of a talk to the California Chamber of Commerce on May 22, 2007. Schwarzenegger often uses this classic line from *The Terminator* (1984) in his speeches.

"When I was on my way to the podium a gentleman stopped me and said I was as good a politician as I was an actor. What a cheap shot."

> — in August 2004 at the 2004 Republican Convention

Calling on voters to rid him of his opponents in the California legislature: "You are the terminators, yes!"

> — in July 2004

"One of my movies was called *True Lies*. And that's what the Democrats should have called their convention."

— in August 2004 at the 2004 Republican convention

About the Republican party: "In movie terms, we are dying at the box office. We are not filling the seats."

— in a Sept. 7, 2007 speech at a GOP convention in California

"To link me to George Bush is like linking me to an Oscar… It's ridiculous."

— in October 2006 on *The Tonight Show*

"To those critics who are so pessimistic about our economy, I say, 'Don't be economic girlie men!'"

— in August 2004 at the 2004 Republican Convention. The disdainful term "girlie men" was a favorite phrase of *Saturday Night Live* characters Hans and Franz, two muscle-bound Arnold worshippers.

EXCUSES
AND RETRACTIONS

Some politicians have a way of wading into hot water when they attempt to justify their behavior or retract what they have said. Here are some of our favorite examples.

Why I Stayed Out of Vietnam

"So many minority youths had volunteered that there was literally no room for patriotic folks like myself."

> — Tom DeLay (R-TX, 1985–2006), speaking at the 1988 Republican National Convention

"Part of the question I had to ask myself was what difference I would have made."

> — Newt Gingrich (R-GA, 1979–99), in an 1985 interview published in *The Wall Street Journal*

★   ★   ★

"Some time around 2:45 a.m., I drove the few blocks to the Capitol Complex believing I needed to vote. Apparently, I was disoriented from the medication."

> — Rep. Patrick Kennedy (D-RI) in a statement about a May 4, 2006 incident. The congressman, who was driving erratically and without headlights, almost hit a police cruiser. During the subsequent chase, Kennedy drove down the wrong side of the road and eventually crashed into a barrier.

"I was trying to escape. Obviously, it didn't work."

> — President George W. Bush in November 2005, explaining why he ended up in a corner trying unsuccessfully to open locked doors. The failed escape attempt took place after a news conference in Beijing. The president had cut the conference short after six questions and then tried to exit the room.

"He didn't say that. He was reading what was given to him in a speech."

> — Richard Darman, director of the Office of Management and Budget, during the first Bush administration, explaining why George H.W. Bush was not following up on his campaign pledge that there would be no loss of wetlands

No Mistakes for You!

President Bush was put on the spot during a Washington press conference in April 2004 when a reporter asked him to name his biggest single mistake since 9/11. "I wish you'd have given me this written question ahead of time so I could plan for it," he quipped. After a pause, he said, "I'm sure something will pop into my head here in the midst of this press conference, with all the pressure of trying to come up with an answer, but it hasn't yet."

Masters of Understatement

"I should have been more vigilant. I should have been more watchful. I should have been a lot of things, I guess."

— George Ryan, former Illinois governor, in September 2006, just before being sentenced to more than six years in prison for accepting bribes and directing state contracts to go to businesses owned by his friends

"I exercised very poor judgment in the course of reviewing the files."

— Sandy Berger, a former Clinton national security advisor, in April 2005 after pleading guilty to a misdemeanor charge of removing classified documents from the National Archives. He hid them under a trailer at a nearby construction site and destroyed several of the files.

Back in June 1989, Rep. Lynn Martin (R-IL) was campaigning for the Illinois senate seat. A journalist asked her to provide a term for Illinois' southern constituents. Martin replied, "Rednecks." Martin herself is from the northern part of Illinois. Later, after much apologizing, she said, "Rednecks are wonderful people. I call myself a redneck."

Let Me Take That Back...

"Last week, *The Hill* erroneously reported that Sen. Larry Presler (R-SD) married his dogs in a mock ceremony, which in fact did not occur."

— a correction in *The Hill*, a Washington-based political newspaper, quoted in the May 1995 *Limbaugh Letter*

LET ME TRY TO
EXPLAIN

Sen. Larry Craig (R-ID) was arrested in June 2007 in a sex sting at an airport men's room and pled guilty. In August 2007, he retracted his guilty plea. An undercover officer had interpreted Craig tapping his foot in his stall as code for soliciting sex. Craig's explanation? His "wide stance" when going to the bathroom.

In an August 2007 forum for Democratic presidential candidates, Bill Richardson called homosexuality a choice. Immediately afterwards, he retracted his statement. His excuse? Jet lag.

During a March 2005 debate about naming the Chuck Wagon the official state vehicle of Texas, state senator Kel Seliger said, "I've already yielded more than a cheerleader at a drive-in." His excuse for his colorful language? "Incipient Tourette's syndrome."

In a Republican candidates' debate in May 2007, Tommy Thompson said that individual companies should be allowed to decide whether to fire homosexual employees, a stance that goes against existing laws. His excuse? Variously, failing to understand the question, a faulty hearing aid, having the flu and needing to go to the bathroom.

AGAINST
POLITICIANS

"What I said was that they'll be scurrying around in Washington just like cockroaches. That is not calling members of Congress cockroaches."

> — Howard Dean, chair of the DNC and former governor of Vermont, in a January 2004 interview

"A politician is a statesman who approaches every question with an open mouth."

> — Adlai Stevenson, former governor of Illinois and U.S. ambassador to the UN

"Presidential ambition is a disease that can only be cured by embalming fluid."

> — Sen. John McCain (R-AZ) in the June 2005 issue of *Men's Journal*

FLASHBACK

"When they call the roll in the Senate, the senators do not know whether to answer 'Present' or 'Not guilty.'"

> — Theodore Roosevelt, 26th president of the United States

ACROSS THE
POND

American politicians don't hold a monopoly on handling the rough waters of politics. Here are a few quotes showing the political mettle of the Brits.

"Being powerful is like being a lady. If you have to tell people you are, you aren't."

> — Margaret Thatcher, nicknamed the "Iron Lady," British prime minister from 1979–90

"A week is a long time in politics."

> — Harold Wilson, British prime minister from 1964–70 and 1974–76

"Politics is more dangerous than war, for in war you are only killed once."

> — Winston Churchill, British prime minister during World War II. Churchill held office from 1940–45 and 1951–55.

FLASHBACK

"Mr. Speaker, I withdraw my statement that half the cabinet are asses. Half the cabinet are not asses."

> — British politician and two-time prime minister Benjamin Disraeli (1804–81), as leader of the opposition

Chapter Three

DOMESTIC ISSUES

TAXES

"Mississippi gets more than their fair share back in federal money, but who the hell wants to live in Mississippi?"

> — Rep. Charles Rangel (D-NY) on Nov. 9, 2006. Rangel later apologized.

As Clear As Mud

In February 2008, John McCain told a rally in Vermont that fixing the "broken tax code" would be one of his first priorities as president. The crowd laughed when he said, "My friends, is there anyone here today that understands our tax code? Please see me afterwards. I'd love to chat with you."

"A recent poll showed that more Americans fear an audit of the IRS than they do getting mugged."

> — former Arkansas governor Mike Huckabee in an August 2007 Republican candidates' debate

"George Bush giving tax cuts is like Jim Jones giving Kool-Aid. It tastes good but it'll kill you."

> — Rev. Al Sharpton in May 2003 at a presidential candidates' debate in Columbia, South Carolina

CHENEY'S GOT A GUN

On Feb. 11, 2006, Vice President Dick Cheney accidentally shot his friend Harry Whittington, a Texas lawyer, in the face during a quail hunt. The incident created controversy because the White House did not immediately reveal details about the shooting to the press. Whittington, who was 78 at the time, suffered a heart attack from a piece of birdshot that migrated to his heart.

Just Imagine How Harry Felt...

"The image of him falling is something I'll never ever be able to get out of my mind. I fired, and there's Harry falling. It was, I'd have to say, one of the worst days of my life at that moment."

— Dick Cheney to Fox News' Brit Hume on Feb. 15, 2006, in his first public statement about the shooting incident

Should *He* Be the One Apologizing?

"My family and I are deeply sorry for all that Vice President Cheney and his family have had to go through this past week."

— Harry Whittington, speaking to reporters on Feb. 17, 2006 as he left the hospital

Taking Pot Shots at the Vice President

The Whittington incident made the vice president the butt of jokes.

Oh, Is *That* What He Meant?

According to *The Washington Post*, Democratic staffers on Capitol Hill took it upon themselves to circulate a quote by President Bush from a 2000 interview with the *Houston Chronicle* where he described Cheney as "somebody who is going to shoot straight with the American people."

Et Tu, George?

At the 2006 Gridiron Club Dinner in March, George W. Bush chipped in with: "I really chewed Dick out for the way he handled the whole thing. I said, 'Dick, I've got an approval rating of 38 percent and you shoot the only trial lawyer in the country who likes me.'"

Sorry, I'm Busy that Day

In fall 2007, it was revealed that Sen. Barack Obama was Dick Cheney's eighth cousin. Obama, during an October 2007 appearance on *The Tonight Show*, told Jay Leno: "The truth is I am okay with it... [but] I don't want to be invited to the family hunting party."

THE ECONOMY

Ah, money. It's what makes the world go round. Here are some thoughts from Washington about the U.S. economy.

"Average folks don't know how to make the economy work."
— **Sen. Joe Biden during a Democratic candidates' debate on June 28, 2007**

During his presidency, Ronald Reagan justified tax cuts with this remark: "I am not worried about the deficit. It is big enough to take care of itself."

"We're enjoying sluggish times, and not enjoying them very much."
— **President George H.W. Bush in 1992**

FLASHBACK

"Recession is when your neighbor loses his job. Depression is when you lose yours. And recovery is when Jimmy Carter loses his."

— **Ronald Reagan in a nod to Harry S. Truman, as a presidential candidate in a 1980 debate against Carter**

GOVERNMENT
SPENDING

Governments are not known for their spending restraint. Perhaps journalist P.J. O'Rourke expressed it best when he said, "Giving government money and power is like giving car keys and whiskey to a teenage boy."

While on a tour in April 2007, Sen. John McCain spoke at a town hall meeting in Des Moines, Iowa about wasteful spending. He noted that he often evokes Ronald Reagan's line about Congress spending money "like a drunken sailor." He added that some people took offense to the comparison. "I'm not making this up when I tell you a few weeks ago I received an e-mail from a guy who said, 'As a former drunken sailor, I resent being compared to members of Congress.'"

"Being lectured by the president on fiscal responsibility is a little bit like Tony Soprano talking to me about law and order in this country."

— Sen. John Kerry, about George W. Bush, during a pre-election debate in fall 2004

About the Democrats: "They want the federal government controlling Social Security like it's some kind of federal program."

— George W. Bush on Nov. 2, 2000, just days before the 2000 election

CRIMINAL THOUGHTS

Forensics May Lose Some of Its Glamour...

"We are using fingerprints, face prints, pretty soon we are going to be using butt prints."

> — Texas state Rep. Garnet Coleman (D-Houston) in 2005, opposing a Texas law requiring residents to provide biometric data to the Department of Public Safety in order to obtain a driver's license

Aiming High...

"My number one goal is to not go to jail."

> — newly elected Rep. Michele Bachmann (R-MN) in November 2006. Bachmann made the quip during an orientation session for new members of Congress.

"There is a sort of an unwritten code in Washington, among the underworld and the hustlers and these other guys, that I am their friend."

> — former mayor and Washington, D.C. council member Marion Barry in 2006, after being robbed at gunpoint in his own apartment

FLASHBACK

"Capital punishment is our society's recognition of the sanctity of human life."

> — Sen. Orrin Hatch in 1988 on the Senate floor, explaining his support of the death penalty

EDJAMUCASHUN

"We're going to have the best-educated American people in
the world."

— Sen. Dan Quayle (R-IN) while campaigning for vice president in 1988

You Write Potato, I Write Potatoe...

Dan Quayle will forever remain notorious for the "potatoe"
incident. On a June 1992 tour of a New Jersey elementary school,
the then-vice president sat in on a spelling bee and told a sixth
grader who'd spelled the word "potato" that it was misspelled
unless he added an "e" to make it "potatoe." The media and
late-night comedians had a field day with the fact that Quayle
was wrong; "potato" only gets an "e" when it's plural. Shortly
afterwards, the student, William Figueroa, appeared as a guest on
Late Night with David Letterman. He told Dave, "I know he's not
an idiot but he needs to study more. Do you have to go to college
to be vice president?" Later, in his 1995 memoir *Standing Firm*,
Quayle showed his sense of humor, writing about the episode in a
chapter that he titled "Baked, Mashed and Fried."

"I have two young daughters who I'm trying to educate them."

— Sen. Christopher Dodd (D-CT), a Democratic presidential hopeful, in
July 2007

"We should replace bilingual education with immersion in English so people learn the common language of the country and they learn the language of prosperity, not the language of living in a ghetto."

> — Newt Gingrich, former House speaker, in March 2007. He later apologized for his remark.

"Childrens" May Learn, But We're Not So Sure About Certain Presidents...

"Is our children learning?"

> — George W. Bush as governor of Texas, campaigning in South Carolina in January 2000

"As yesterday's positive report card shows, childrens do learn when standards are high and results are measured."

> — President George W. Bush in September 2007, at an event where he praised improved test scores among primary school children

JOBS, JOBS, JOBS

Any Plans to Help the *Un*employed?

"I will make sure that everyone who has a job wants a job."

— Vice President George H.W. Bush while campaigning for president in 1988

Please Don't Try Too Hard

"We are trying to get unemployment to go up, and I think we're going to succeed."

— Ronald Reagan, at a GOP fundraising dinner in 1982

Is That What "Competitive Economy" Means?

"It's a game where trade deals like NAFTA ship jobs overseas and force parents to compete with their teenagers to work for minimum wage at Wal-Mart."

— Sen. Barack Obama (D-IL) in a February 2008 speech in Madison, Wisconsin

About jobs going to Mexico: "You're going to hear a giant sucking sound going south."

— independent presidential candidate Ross Perot in 1992. Perot garnered 19% of the popular vote in the '92 election.

ENVIRONMENT

Wit Ambrose Bierce defines "out-of-doors" as "that part of one's environment upon which no government has been able to collect taxes." Here's what the politicians have to say about our relationship with nature.

"In Alabama we have had experience turning corn into alcohol for years."

> — Bob Riley, governor of Alabama, in June 2007, joking about the state's tradition of moonshining. Riley made the quip while announcing that the state's fleet of cars would switch to ethanol-based fuel.

"Excuse me, but can someone please explain what an ecosystem is?"

> — Rep. Helen Chenoweth (R-ID, 1995–2001) on the House floor

"It is so bad, if a dog urinates in a parking lot, the EPA declares it a wetland. Beam me up, Mr. Speaker."

> — Rep. James Traficant (D-OH, 1985–2002)

FLASHBACK

"A tree is a tree. How many more do you need to look at?"

— Ronald Reagan in 1966 as governor of California, opposing the expansion of Redwoods Park

"I think the presidency ought to be held at a higher level than having to answer questions from a snowman."

> — Mitt Romney, GOP party hopeful, in July 2007, referring to a CNN debate in which an online participant delivered a question about global warming while dressed as a snowman

"Republicans will save the rain forest if you tell them that's where the golf ball trees are."

> — journalist P.J. O'Rourke

Like Father, Like Son

"If you're worried about the caribou, take a look at the arguments that were used about the pipeline. They'd say the caribou would be extinct. You've got to shake them away with a stick. They're all making love lying up against the pipeline, and you've got thousands of caribou up there."

> — President George H.W. Bush in 1991, about the Alaskan Pipeline

"I know that human being and fish can co-exist peacefully."

> — George W. Bush, then-governor of Texas, campaigning in Michigan in September 2000

GUNS

During a July 2007 Democratic debate, questions were posed by everyday citizens via YouTube. One voter asked about gun control, saying, "Tell me your position on gun control, as myself and other Americans really want to know if our babies are safe." He then pulled out an automatic weapon and said, "This is my baby." Sen. Joe Biden (D-DE) responded, "I'll tell you what, if that is his baby, he needs help." Biden later added, "I don't know that he's mentally qualified to own that gun."

Birth Control Causes Juvenile Violence?

"Guns have little or nothing to do with juvenile violence. The causes of youth violence are working parents who put their kids into daycare, the teaching of evolution in the schools, and working mothers who take birth control pills."

— Tom DeLay as a Texas congressman, in 1999

"I don't hunt, myself, but I respect hunters and sportsmen. But I don't know of any self-respecting hunter that needs 19 rounds of anything. You don't shoot 19 rounds at a deer, and if you do, you shouldn't be hunting."

— Sen. Barack Obama on April 20, 2007

About gun control: "They even turned down a law in many states that the proposition was that you could only buy one gun a month. And this was too much of a slippery slope for some people. One a month. 'What about Christmas?' they said. 'What about my gun-of-the-month club? You get that thirteenth extra.' If you started when you were 18 and collected till you were 60, that would be over 500 guns. Now, I don't care how small your penis is, Larry, you don't need that many guns."

— **Bill Maher to Larry King, on** *Larry King Live*

"I'm by no means a big game hunter. I'm more Jed Clampett than Teddy Roosevelt."

— **former Massachusetts governor Mitt Romney in April 2007, clarifying his relationship with guns. Romney found himself being dissected by the press after he described himself as a life-long hunter.**

"I own a couple of guns—but I'm not going to tell you what they are or where they are."

— **former senator and 2008 presidential hopeful Fred Thompson in November 2007, at a Republican candidates' debate in Florida**

WHEN DISASTER
STRIKES

After Hurricane Katrina, Congressional Democrats called for the firing of FEMA head Michael Brown. Nancy Pelosi (D-CA, 1987–) related a discussion she had with President George W. Bush in the week after Katrina hit. She said the president's response to the call to sack Brown was, "Why would I do that?" Pelosi reported. "I said because of all that went wrong, of all that didn't go right last week. And he said, 'What didn't go right?'" At that point, devastation from the hurricane had caused more than $80 billion damage along the Gulf Coast and killed more than 1,800 people.

★   ★   ★

Evacuation... or Vacation?

Referring to Katrina evacuees: "What I'm hearing, which is sort of scary, is they all want to stay in Texas. Everyone is so overwhelmed by the hospitality. And so many of the people in the arena here, you know, were underprivileged anyway, so this is working very well for them."

— former first lady Barbara Bush in September 2005, after touring Houston's Astrodome

"Now tell me the truth, boys, is this kind of fun?"

— Rep. Tom DeLay (R-TX, 1985–2006) in September 2005 to three youths evacuated from New Orleans after Hurricane Katrina, while they were camped out in emergency shelters in Houston

"In case you missed it, this week, there was a tragedy in Kansas. Ten thousand people died—an entire town destroyed."

> — Sen. Barack Obama (D-IL) in Virginia in May 2007. Obama was criticizing the depletion of the National Guard due to the Iraq War and its inability to respond to a tornado in Greensburg. The actual death toll was 12 in the town of 1,574.

Disaster Photo Op?

"Get some devastation in the back."

> — Senate majority leader Sen. Bill Frist (R-TN, 1995–2007) in January 2005, in an area of Sri Lanka affected by the Indian Ocean tsunami. Frist was speaking to an aide who was taking photos.

It's *All* Good News?

When wildfires started burning in southern California in October 2007, half a million people evacuated their homes. San Diego's Qualcomm Stadium served as one of the evacuation centers, housing thousands of people. Gov. Arnold Schwarzenegger toured the stadium on Oct. 24, and spoke with the evacuees. ABC News asked the governor how this evacuation compared with Katrina. Arnie replied, "All you have to do is just look around here and see how happy people are. They're sitting here, and they're happy... They're getting tutoring for their kids, and they're getting their yoga classes, and they're getting their food and their diapers." He added, "Trust me when I tell you, you're looking for a mistake and you won't find it, because it's all good news."

Chapter Four

FOREIGN
AFFAIRS

FOREIGN POLICY

John F. Kennedy once said, "Domestic policy can only defeat us; foreign policy can kill us." Here are some examples of how well politicians deal with the world outside the United States.

Of This, We Are Absolutely Sure...

"We do know of certain knowledge that he is either in Afghanistan, or in some other country, or dead."

> — **Defense Secretary Donald Rumsfeld in December 2001, showcasing his dry wit while talking about the whereabouts of Osama bin Laden, one of the founders of the terrorist group al Qaeda**

"Bill Clinton's foreign policy experience is pretty much limited to having had breakfast once at the International House of Pancakes."

> — **political advisor Pat Buchanan, a Republican presidential hopeful in the 1992 and 1996 elections, at the 1992 Republican National Convention**

About how he would handle foreign trade: "I would immediately call the president of Mexico, the president of Canada, to try to amend NAFTA, because I think that we can get labor agreements in that agreement right now."

> — **Sen. Barack Obama in an August 2007 debate. Canada has a prime minister, not a president.**

Andy Hiller of WHDH-TV in Boston asked then-Texas governor
George W. Bush to name the leaders of Taiwan, Chechnya, India,
and Pakistan.

> BUSH: "Wait, wait, is this 50 questions?"
>
> HILLER: "No, it's four questions of four
> leaders in four hot spots."

Bush could not name the leaders of any of the four countries.

According to the U.S. State Department, only 10 of the 1,000
employees at the U.S. Embassy in Baghdad have a working
knowledge of Arabic.

George W. Bush made his first official visit to Canada in
November 2004. He was greeted by both supporters and
protesters. Some of the latter expressed their displeasure by
greeting the president with the finger. During a press conference,
he said, "I want to thank the Canadian people who came out to
wave—with all five fingers—for their hospitality."

"American diplomacy. It's like watching somebody trying to do
joinery with a chainsaw."

— **English writer James Hamilton-Paterson in *Griefwork* (1993)**

In December 2002, a congressman suggested to President George W. Bush that the Swedish army might be a good choice for peacekeeping forces in the West Bank and Gaza strip. Bush replied, "I don't know why you're talking about Sweden. They're the neutral one. They don't have an army." In fact, Switzerland is the country known for its neutrality. Both Switzerland and Sweden have well-trained armed forces.

The Not-So-United Nations

"The Secretariat building in New York has 38 stories. If you lost 10 stories today, it wouldn't make a bit of difference."

> — John Bolton in a Feb. 3, 1994 speech in New York City. Bolton later went on to serve as the U.S. representative to the United Nations.

"If I were redoing the Security Council today, I'd have one permanent member because that's the real reflection of the distribution of power in the world … the United States."

> — John Bolton on public radio in 2000

"We should use the UN for what it is good for. It offers credibility… We can use the UN in Iraq to help spread the blame around—let them hate some French and others, instead of hating just us."

> — Wesley Clark, retired U.S. Army general, in September 2003 before throwing his hat in the ring for Democratic presidential nomination

IRAQ WAR

"If the president wants to go to war, our job is to find the intelligence to allow him to do so."

> — Alan Foley, head of the CIA's Weapons Intelligence Non-Proliferation and Arms Control Center, in December 2002

"You know, one of the hardest parts of my job is to connect Iraq to the war on terror."

> — President George W. Bush to Katie Couric in a Sept. 6, 2006 interview

"It's hard for me, you know, living in this beautiful White House, to give you a firsthand assessment."

> — President George W. Bush in February 2007, on how the U.S. was doing in Iraq

---

FLASHBACK

"My fellow Americans, I'm pleased to tell you today that I've signed legislation that will outlaw Russia forever. We begin bombing in five minutes."

> — President Ronald Reagan on Aug. 11, 1984 before his weekly radio address; Reagan was joking around during a sound check. Neither he nor the sound technician realized the remark was being broadcast. The incident strained Soviet relations and caused a drop in Reagan's popularity.

Sen. John McCain (R-AZ) made headlines in March 2007 after he told radio host Bill Bennett how calm the city of Baghdad was. McCain, who was part of a congressional delegation to Iraq, told Bennett on *Morning in America*, "There are neighborhoods in Baghdad where you and I could walk through...today."

In reaction, CNN's Baghdad correspondent Michael Ware told Wolf Blitzer that the idea "that there's any neighborhood in this city where an American can walk freely is beyond ludicrous." He added, "I'd love Sen. McCain to tell me where that neighborhood is, and he and I can go for a stroll."

The *New York Times* reported that, during the delegation's hour-long visit to a Baghdad market, the group was accompanied by more than 100 soldiers in armored vehicles, as well as attack helicopters circling overhead. The congressmen themselves wore bulletproof vests.

They Should Be Grateful

"They're very well-treated down there. They're living in the tropics."

> — Vice President Dick Cheney in June 2005, about detainees at the Guantanamo detention facility

"I can tell you, most of our prisoners would love to be in a facility more like Guantanamo and less like the state prisons that people are in in the United States."

> — 2008 presidential hopeful Mike Huckabee in June 2007, on CNN's *Late Edition*

John Kerry on Iraq

Ever the Decisive Leader

Sen. John Kerry (D-MA) in August 2004, on whether his administration would have gone to war against Iraq if Saddam Hussein had refused to disarm: "You bet we might have."

"I actually did vote for the $87 billion before I voted against it."

— Sen. John Kerry, responding to a 2004 ad accusing him of voting against additional funding for the Iraq war

Open Mouth, Insert Foot

"Education, if you make the most of it, you study hard and you do your homework and you make an effort to be smart, you can do well. If not, you get stuck in Iraq."

— Sen. John Kerry in October 2006 to a group of college students. Kerry claims he meant to criticize Bush by saying "you get *us* stuck in Iraq," but misspoke.

"He was for the joke before he was against it."

— Vice President Dick Cheney, socking it to John Kerry for his "stuck in Iraq" blunder, in November 2006

"My opponent clearly has strong beliefs. They just don't last very long."

— President George W. Bush at a March 2004 luncheon in Dallas, Texas, referring to Democratic presidential nominee John Kerry

IS ANYONE ELSE
DISTURBED
BY THIS?

These comments make for powerful rhetoric, but, as the saying goes, you should be careful what you wish for.

We're Glad It's Not up to You

"If it is up to me, we are going to explain that an attack on this homeland of that nature would be followed by an attack on the holy sites in Mecca and Medina."

> — Rep. Tom Tancredo (R-CO), a GOP presidential nomination contender, speaking in August 2007 on how he would deter a future nuclear attack on the United States

"A really ruthless al Qaeda- or Hamas-style attack—a dirty bomb at Disneyworld, something of that sort—would unleash the furies that woke, but did not take wing, after 9/11."

> — *National Review* columnist John Derbyshire in a June 2003 column

"At the end of the day, I believe fully the president is doing the right thing, and I think all we need are some attacks on American soil like we had on [Sept. 11, 2001], and the naysayers will come around very quickly."

> — Dennis Milligan, head of the Arkansas GOP, quoted in the *Arkansas Democrat Gazette* on June 3, 2007

WHEN DO WE
LEAVE?

After the U.S. invaded Iraq on March 20, 2003, critics began asking, "When do we leave?" The answers have evolved over time.

"Vietnam? You think you have to tell me about Vietnam? Of course it won't be Vietnam. We are going to go in, overthrow Saddam, get out. That's it."

> — Defense Secretary Donald Rumsfeld early on in the conflict, in response to comments from Air Force secretary Jim Roche. The exchange was reported in *Newsweek* in November 2006.

"It is unknowable how long that conflict will last. It could last six days, six weeks. I doubt six months."

> — Defense Secretary Donald Rumsfeld in February 2003

"I think they're in the last throes, if you will, of the insurgency."

> — Vice President Dick Cheney in a June 2005 interview with Larry King

About the Republicans: "They like this war. They want this war to continue."

> — House Speaker Rep. Nancy Pelosi (D-CA) in December 2007

On Course

Here are some of George W. Bush's responses.

Dec. 15, 2003:
"We're just going to stay the course."

April 5, 2004:
"But we will stay the course. We will do what is right."

April 16, 2004:
"It's a wonderful feeling to have a strong ally in believing in the power of free societies and liberty. And that's why we're going to stay the course in Iraq."

Aug. 4, 2005:
"We will stay the course. We will complete the job in Iraq."

Aug. 30, 2006:
"We will stay the course, we will help this young Iraqi democracy succeed, and victory in Iraq will be a major ideological triumph in the struggle of the 21st century."

Oct. 22, 2006:
Speaking to George Stephanopoulos: "Well, hey, listen, we've never been 'stay the course,' George."

WEAPONS
OF MASS DESTRUCTION

The Bush administration told us emphatically and repeatedly that it had found evidence of WMDs in Iraq. The fact that there was no evidence is a gaffe that haunts George W. Bush's presidency.

"We know where they are. They're in the area around Tikrit and Baghdad and east, west, south and north somewhat."

> — Defense Secretary Donald Rumsfeld on the location of Iraq's weapons of mass destruction, on March 30, 2003

"I think the burden is on those people who think he didn't have weapons of mass destruction to tell the world where they are."

> — spokesman Ari Fleischer in a White House briefing, on July 9, 2003

Evidence, Schmevidence

"We now have irrefutable evidence."

> — Vice President Dick Cheney on Sept. 20, 2002. He was talking about Saddam Hussein acquiring "nuclear use" aluminum tubes made of the same material used in U.S. Air Force's air-to-ground rocket tubes.

"I did misspeak.... We never had any evidence that he had acquired a nuclear weapon."

> — Dick Cheney on Sept. 14, 2003, approximately six months after the U.S. invaded Iraq

IMMIGRATION

Asked by a journalist which issue is most important to Iowans during the Ames straw poll, Rep. Duncan Hunter responded, "The border is most important, I think, to Iowans." The U.S.–Mexico border is more than 1,100 miles away from Ames.

"In Delaware, the largest growth in population is Indian-Americans moving from India. You cannot go to a 7-Eleven or a Dunkin' Donuts unless you have a slight Indian accent. I'm not joking."
> — Sen. Joe Biden (D-DE) on C-SPAN's *Road to the White House* in June 2006

In March 2006, Michael Bloomberg, New York City mayor, was asked by WABC radio host John Gambling what he thought of illegal immigration. Bloomberg responded: "You and I both play golf. Who takes care of the greens and the fairways in your golf course?"

"Twelve million illegal immigrants later, we are now living in a nation that is beset by people who are suicidal maniacs and want to kill countless innocent men, women and children around the world."
> — Fred Thompson, Republican presidential candidate, in 2007

Chapter Five

AMERICAN VALUES

GENDER

"We've got an awful lot of members that don't understand that harass is one word, not two."

— Rep. Patricia Schroeder (D-CO, 1973–97) about being a woman in Congress, on *Politics With Chris Matthews* in 1996

"If combat means living in a ditch, females have biological problems staying in a ditch for 30 days because they get infections… On the other hand, if combat means being on an Aegis class cruiser managing the computer controls for twelve ships, a female may be again dramatically better than a male, who gets very, very frustrated sitting in a chair all the time because males are biologically driven to go out and hunt giraffes."

— Newt Gingrich (R-GA, 1979–99) in January 1995, speaking to students at Reinhardt College

Describing John Roberts: "[He is a] brilliant legal mind, a straight shooter, articulate, and he should not have trouble being confirmed by October. He's good in every way, except he's not a woman."

— Supreme Court justice Sandra Day O'Connor in July 2005, about soon-to-be Supreme Court chief justice John Roberts

LET'S TALK ABOUT
SEX, BABY

There is an old piece of political advice that goes, "Never get caught in bed with a dead woman or a live man." Sex is certainly one of Washington's favorite topics, whether politicians are talking about their own values or the latest scandal.

"The Clinton administration was the best years for the adult industry."

> — Jenna Jameson in a May 17, 2007 interview. Jameson is an adult film star and author of the best-seller *How to Make Love like a Porn Star* (2004).

"What's a man got to do to get in the top fifty?"

> — President Bill Clinton, in 1999. He was reacting to a survey of national journalists that ranked the Monica Lewinsky scandal as the 53rd most significant story of the century.

Mitt Romney, presidential hopeful for 2008, tells a story about turning to his wife before the Salt Lake City Games were about to begin and saying, "Did you ever in your wildest dreams imagine that we'd be here at the Olympics?" She replied, "Mitt, you weren't in my wildest dreams."

In March 2005, Texas state Rep. Al Edwards (D-Houston) introduced a bill banning sexually suggestive cheerleading. He said he introduced the bill so that youths would stop receiving mixed messages. "We say to them, 'Don't get involved in sex unless it's marriage or love, it's dangerous out there,' and yet the teachers and directors are helping them go through those kind of gyrations." Asked what he meant by sexually suggestive cheerleading, Edwards said, "I can't define yours for you or you define mine for me. I don't have a word-for-word description of it, but any adult who is involved with sex at all in their life—they know it when they see it. I can't give you a demonstration this evening."

"Boys were allowed in our rooms only on Sunday afternoons. And we had to observe what was called then the two-feet rule. That meant two out of four feet had to be on the floor at all times. Try it sometime!"

— Sen. Hillary Clinton in a November 2007 speech at Wellesley College

While dressed as Barney the dinosaur at a Christmas party, Sen. Ted Kennedy declared, "They don't call me Tyrannosaurus Sex for nothing."

HOMOSEXUALITY

Brothers in Arms?

"If you have any knowledge of history—ancient history—in Sparta, they encouraged homosexuality because they fight for the people they love, and if it's your partner and you love him, then you're prepared to die for him. It's the same ethic in the military today. It's not the country—it's my partner who's sharing my foxhole with me."

— former senator Mike Gravel (D-AK) in February 2007, on why he supports gays in the military

Phantom Menace?

"Lesbianism is so rampant in some of the schools in southeast Oklahoma that they'll only let one girl go to the bathroom. Now think about it."

— soon-to-be senator Tom Coburn (R-OK) during his 2004 Senate race, recounting what a campaign worker from Coalgate, Oklahoma told him. He had apparently meant to say "one girl at a time." School officials said this was not an issue.

THE POLITICS OF
MARRIAGE

During an appearance at the Panetta Institute in October 2004, California's Governor Arnold Schwarzenegger, a Republican, gave the audience some insight into his marriage with Democrat Maria Shriver. When asked how his wife had reacted to his recent speech in support of George W. Bush at the Republican National Convention, he replied, "Well, there was no sex for 14 days. Everything comes with side effects." Later, he said: "I don't even know why I should watch the presidential debates. If I want to see a liberal Democrat—a smart, liberal Democrat—and a Republican leader argue, we just go out for dinner." He added, "Fortunately for Bush and Kerry, they were lucky they only had to [debate] three times. I have to do it every morning when I get up."

"In France, for instance, I'm told that marriage is now frequently contracted in seven-year terms where either party may move on when their term is up. How shallow and how different from the Europe of the past."

— Mitt Romney, former governor of Massachusetts and GOP presidential hopeful, in May 2007. *Time* magazine, in an article on Romney, notes that such a policy does not exist in France. France does have civil union agreements, but they have no set end date.

"I'll do whatever she wants, and I have no idea what that is."

> — former president Bill Clinton in 2006, explaining his role if his wife Hillary Clinton ran in and won the 2008 presidential election

Wanted: Companion for Long Walks on the Beach and Discussions About the Economy

During a 2003 Democratic presidential nomination contenders' forum on women's issues, Rep. Dennis Kucinich (D-OH) said, "As a bachelor, I get a chance to fantasize about my first lady," and that he was looking for "a dynamic, outspoken woman who was fearless in her desire for peace in the world and for universal single-payer health care and a full employment economy." He told the crowd, "If you are out there, call me." The political Web site NHPolitics.com began taking personal ads for the Ohio congressman. Kucinich took himself off the market in 2005.

"Buddy, the dog, came along to keep Bill company... He was the only member of our family who was still willing to."

> — Sen. Hillary Clinton in her 2003 book, *Living History*, about the Lewinsky scandal

THOUGHTS ON SAME-SEX
MARRIAGE

"Dear friends, until Moses comes down with two stone tablets from Brokeback Mountain saying we've changed the rules, let's keep it like it is."

— Mike Huckabee, former governor of Arkansas and 2008 presidential hopeful, speaking about gay marriage at the Values Voter Summit in Washington in September 2006

"If you ask yourself the question, 'How would you like your children treated if they had a different sexual orientation than their parents?' the answer is yes."

— Christopher Dodd in July 2007, not quite answering the question about whether he supports same-sex marriages

In August 2007, gay rights group Human Rights Campaign and the TV Channel Logo offered to host forums for presidential candidates from each party to discuss gay and lesbian issues. Who took advantage of the offer? On the Democratic side, almost all of the candidates showed up, including front-runners Barack Obama, Hillary Clinton, and John Edwards. And the Republican forum? Canceled due to lack of interest.

"I think that gay marriage should be between a man and a woman."

> — Arnold Schwarzenegger, while campaigning for governor of California in 2003

"I believe marriage should be between a man and a woman...and a woman...and a woman."

> — Mitt Romney, the lone Mormon politician running for the GOP candidacy in 2008. He used this quip in 2005 and again in 2006 on Don Imus' St. Patrick's Day show.

"Should Mitt Romney join a 2008 race that included John McCain, Rudy Giuliani, Newt Gingrich and George Allen, the only guy in the GOP field with only one wife would be the Mormon."

> — Kate O'Beirne, Washington editor of *The National Review*, writing in August 2006

"I don't think anybody should get married."

> — divorced New York City mayor Michael Bloomberg, responding to questions about same-sex marriage

IF YOU LIVE IN A
GLASS HOUSE...

Carl Jung once said, "Everything that irritates us about others can lead us to an understanding about ourselves." Maybe these two Bill Clinton critics know what he means.

"The Senate certainly can bring about a censure resolution, and it's a slap on the wrist. It's a, 'Bad boy, Bill Clinton, you're a naughty boy.' The American people already know that Bill Clinton is a bad boy, a naughty boy. I'm going to speak out for the citizens of my state who in the majority think that Bill Clinton is probably even a nasty, bad, naughty boy."

> — Sen. Larry Craig (R-ID) on *Meet the Press*, Jan. 24, 1999. In August 2007, Craig faced allegations of soliciting gay sex in a Minneapolis airport bathroom.

"It's vile. It's more sad than anything else, to see someone with such potential throw it all down the drain because of a sexual addiction."

> — Rep. Mark Foley (R-FL) about Bill Clinton, in 1998. Foley resigned from Congress in September 2006 after he was implicated in a sex scandal involving minors who had served as congressional pages. Foley had served as the chair of the committee House Caucus on Missing and Exploited Children.

RACE

"Why do they hate each other? Why do Sunnis kill Shiites? How do they tell the difference? They all look the same to me."

— Sen. Trent Lott (R-MS) in September 2006

"I want to say this about my state: when Strom Thurmond ran for president, we voted for him. We're proud of it. And if the rest of the country had followed our lead, we wouldn't have had all these problems over all these years, either."

— Republican Senate leader Sen. Trent Lott in December 2002. A controversy immediately erupted; Thurmond's 1948 campaign had included this sentiment: "All the laws of Washington and all the bayonets of the Army cannot force the Negro into our homes, our schools, our churches." Lott apologized and resigned his Senate leadership.

"You think the Republican National Committee could get this many people of color in a single room? Only if they had the hotel staff in here."

— DNC chairman Howard Dean at a Feb. 11, 2005 meeting with the Congressional Black Caucus

"You know, when I'm catching a cab in Manhattan—in the past, I think I've given my credentials."

— Sen. Barack Obama (D-IL) about whether he was "authentically black," at a July 2007 Democratic candidates' debate

Biden Puts Foot in Mouth

The Blooper

About Barack Obama: "I mean, you got the first mainstream African-American who is articulate and bright and clean and a nice-looking guy. I mean, that's a storybook, man."

— Sen. Joe Biden (D-DE) quoted in the Jan. 31 *New York Observer*, the same day Biden announced his candidacy for the Democratic presidential nomination. Some black leaders found the comment racially insensitive.

Obama Responds

"I didn't take Sen. Biden's comments personally, but obviously they were historically inaccurate. African-American presidential candidates like Jesse Jackson, Shirley Chisholm, Carol Moseley Braun and Al Sharpton gave a voice to many important issues through their campaigns, and no one would call them inarticulate."

— Sen. Barack Obama (D-IL) in a statement released the same day

Sharpton Wades In

What he said to Biden when Biden called to apologize: "I told him I take a bath every day."

— Rev. Al Sharpton to reporters on Jan. 31, 2007

Chapter Six

IN THE PUBLIC EYE

LOOKING GOOD

In 1993, shortly after winning a populist "Putting People First" campaign, President Bill Clinton held up air traffic at Los Angeles International Airport while he received a $200 haircut from Hollywood stylist Christophe in Air Force One on the tarmac.

After John Kerry had bungled a question concerning his favorite Red Sox player in October 2004, Rudolph Giuliani quipped, "You can't really read the sports pages when you're getting a manicure."

Beverly Hills hair stylist Joseph Torrenueva was paid $1,250 by the 2008 John Edwards campaign for a haircut in Atlanta. "He has nice hair," Torrenueva said in July 2007. "I try to make the man handsome, strong, more mature." Edwards also twice paid $400 for haircuts in Iowa, listing them both as campaign expenses. A popular Internet video made fun of the attention Edwards gives to his hair, showing a stylist fussing over him for more than two minutes while the song "I Feel Pretty" played in the background.

"We've had a Congress that's spent money like John Edwards at a beauty shop."
— Mike Huckabee on May 15, 2007

In July 2006, the day before giving a presentation to the "American Dream Initiative," Sen. Hillary Clinton paid nearly $3,000 for hairstyling and makeup. Her campaign paid for it and justified doing so saying it was a media presentation expense.

About Hillary Clinton: "I admire what Sen. Clinton has done for America, what her husband did for America. I'm not sure about that coat."

> — Democratic presidential hopeful John Edwards in a July 2007 debate. Edwards had been asked to name one thing he liked and one thing he disliked about Sen. Clinton.

"People tell me that Sen. Edwards got picked for his good looks, his sex appeal and his great hair. I say to them, 'How do you think I got the job?'"

> — Vice President Dick Cheney at the 2004 RNC convention in September 2004. Edwards had been chosen as John Kerry's running mate for the 2004 election.

FLASHBACK

"Ronald Reagan's hair color was somewhere between a blue-bruise and Shinola, but—hey!—he was 70-something. And his roots didn't exactly tap into Grade-A topsoil... so he needed all the help he could get."

> — political commentator and radio personality Jim Hightower in 1993

POP!
GOES THE WEASEL

Here's a collection of quotes showing politicians doing what they do best—giving slippery answers to tough questions, a.k.a. using weasel words.

"I was not lying. I said things that later on seemed to be untrue."

> — former president Richard Nixon, talking about Watergate in a 1978 TV interview with David Frost

In 1996, then-senator Bob Dole, a presidential nominee, was asked if American lives were more important than foreign lives. He replied, "Life is very important to Americans."

When asked in July 2007 to comment on whether America's progress in Iraq would receive a failing grade, Condoleezza Rice, U.S. secretary of state, said, "I don't agree that you would give it a failing grade. I would say you would say it was a work in progress and you would say that they have made not inconsequential movement forward on some of the important benchmarks."

"Needless to say, the president is correct. Whatever it was he said."
— Defense Secretary Donald Rumsfeld in 2003

"If I seem unduly clear to you, you must have misunderstood what I said."
— Federal Reserve chairman Alan Greenspan, speaking to a Senate committee in 1987

Pat Buchanan, a political analyst for MSNBC, gave us a lesson in splitting hairs in a January 2006 exchange with Chris Matthews on *Hardball with Chris Matthews*. Matthews asked Buchanan if wiretapping residents was wrong. Buchanan replied that what the National Security Agency was doing was not wiretapping. Rather, he said, it was eavesdropping. When Matthews asked him to explain the distinction, he replied, "The difference is you're not putting a wire, going over somebody's stuff. What they're doing is picking this stuff out of the air and going through it. It's eavesdropping."

"There are things we know, and we know we know them—the known knowns. There are things we know that we don't know—the known unknowns. And there are unknown unknowns; the things we do not yet know that we do not know."
— Donald Rumsfeld, during a department of defense briefing in 2002

Heinous Crimes and Punishment

The Associated Press asked the 2004 Democratic presidential candidates whether they supported capital punishment. We noticed that great minds seem to think an awful lot alike.

"I believe the death penalty should be available for extreme and heinous crimes ... But it must be carried out with scrupulous fairness."

— Howard Dean

"I believe the death penalty is the most fitting punishment for the most heinous crimes, and I support it. But we need reforms in the death penalty to ensure that defendants receive fair trials."

— John Edwards

"I believe the death penalty should be available for the most heinous crimes. At the same time, I am concerned about reports of mistakes on death row, and errors and unfairness in our criminal justice system."

— Wesley Clark

"I support the death penalty for heinous crimes, but I also believe we have the responsibility to ensure that it is enforced in a manner that is fair and just."

— Dick Gephardt

MANGLED, MUDDLED AND
MIXED-UP WORDS

Yeah, I'm Having the Same Problem...

"Too many good docs are getting out of business. Too many OB-GYNs aren't able to practice their love with women all across this country."

— President George W. Bush, during the 2004 presidential campaign

Uh, You Meant "Intelligence," Right?

"I am not going to give you a number for it because it is not my job to do intelligent work."

— Donald Rumsfeld, after being asked to estimate the number of Iraqi insurgents while testifying before Congress on Feb.16, 2005

"We can build a collective civic space large enough for all our separate identities, that we can be *e pluribus unum*—out of one, many."

— Vice President Al Gore, speaking in Milwaukee in January 1994. The Latin motto of the United States actually translates to "out of many, one."

"Machismo gracias."

> — Vice President Al Gore in response to applause at the start of a speech given to a largely Hispanic audience in Albuquerque, New Mexico in 1996. While he was probably trying to say "muchas gracias," what he said translates to "manliness, thanks."

"They have miscalculated me as a leader."

> — George W. Bush, campaigning in California in September 2000

"I'm incontinent with joy."

> — Republican Florida state senate hopeful Andy Martin in 1996 after hearing the other Republican nominees had dropped out of the running, in an interview with the *Fort Myers News-Press*

"I rule nothing in or nothing out."

> — President George W. Bush in July 2007, about whether he planned to grant a full pardon to Lewis "Scooter" Libby days before commuting his 30-month sentence

---

FLASHBACK

"I resent your insinuendos."

> — long-time Chicago mayor Richard J. Daley. Known for his unique English styling, he governed the city from 1955–76 and was involved in the Democratic Party at the federal level. Another classic Daley remark is, "No man is an Ireland."

I Have Some Bad News for You, Elizabeth

"Only one thing would be worse than the status quo. And that would be for the status quo to become the norm."

> — Elizabeth Dole in 1999, while campaigning for the Republican presidential nomination

"Facts are stupid things."

> — President Ronald Reagan at the 1988 Republican National Convention. He was attempting to quote John Adams' line, "Facts are *stubborn* things."

From Beyond the Grave...

Do They Talk Back?

"I talk to those who've lost their lives, and they have that sense of duty and mission."

> — Sen. Jeff Sessions (R-AL) in December 2006, about the troops

"Those who survived the San Francisco earthquake said, 'Thank God, I'm still alive.' But, of course, those who died, their lives will never be the same again."

> — Sen. Barbara Boxer (D-CA) in May 1996

JOKING ABOUT
ONESELF

Politicians are often the butt of jokes made by opponents, critics and comedians. Some of them show their sense of humor and make jokes at their own expense.

"We don't all agree on everything. I don't agree with myself on everything."

> — Rudolph Giuliani, former New York City mayor, while campaigning as a Republican presidential candidate in 2007

Delaware's Sen. Joe Biden had put his foot in mouth several times in 2007 while campaigning as a Democratic presidential candidate. Later, in a conversation on *The Daily Show* in August 2007, Biden mentioned that his son Beau Biden was Delaware's attorney general. Host Jon Stewart asked him if there was anything in Delaware that was not controlled by the Biden family. Biden laughed and replied, "Yes, me. My mouth. My ability to not get in trouble."

FLASHBACK

"This is the worst disaster in California since I was elected."

— Pat Brown, governor of California from 1959–67, referring to a local flood

"A year ago, my approval rating was in the 30s, my nominee for the Supreme Court had just withdrawn, and my vice president had shot someone. Ahhh, those were the good old days."

> — President George W. Bush in March 2007 at the White House Correspondents' Dinner

"I'm probably the only one who gets mailings from AARP and diaper services."

> — Christopher Dodd, Connecticut senator and Democratic presidential candidate for 2008. He said this in 2007, when he was 63 and his two daughters were 5 and 2.

"I'm always working on new material because my wife says my old material stinks."

> — Mike Huckabee, former governor of Arkansas and Republican presidential candidate, in June 2007, about his jokes

At a GOP debate hosted by ABC News in August 2007, moderator George Stephanopoulos asked each candidate to answer the question, "What is a defining mistake of your life and why?" When it came to his turn, Rudy Giuliani quipped, "A description of my mistakes in 30 seconds?" and shook his head.

"I'm not into this detail stuff. I'm more concepty."

— Defense Secretary Donald Rumsfeld in a Jan. 9, 2002 interview with *The Washington Post*

In April 2006, Sen. Barack Obama (D-IL) gave a speech at Washington's Gridiron Club. He concluded with this remark directed at the media, "Most of all, I want to thank you for all the generous advance coverage you've given me in anticipation of a successful career. When I actually do something, we'll let you know." Afterwards, at the same dinner, President Bush said, "Sen. Obama, I wanted to do a joke on you, but it's like doing a joke on the Pope." He added, "Give me some material to work with here. You know, mispronounce something."

"I can self-destruct in one sentence... Sometimes in one word."

— Sen. Conrad Burns (R-MT) during his 2006 Senate campaign, recognizing his tendency to make controversial comments. Burns did not win his bid for re-election.

> **FLASHBACK**
>
> During the famous 1858 Lincoln-Douglas debates when Abraham Lincoln first ran for senator, Stephen Douglas attacked his opponent for being two-faced. Lincoln replied, "If I had another face, do you think that I would use this one?"

YOU DON'T SAY:
STATING THE OBVIOUS

Known for pretty rhetoric, politicians sometimes don't worry about whether they are saying anything earth-shattering.

"Youth lacks, to some extent, experience."
> — Spiro Agnew, 39th vice president of the United States

"Things are more like they are now than they ever were before."
> — Dwight Eisenhower, 34th president of the United States

"When more and more people are thrown out of work, unemployment results."
> — Calvin Coolidge, 30th president of the United States

"We'll succeed unless we quit."
> — President George W. Bush in November 2006 on the lesson he learned from the Vietnam War and that he applies to Iraq

TECHNOLOGY

George Dubya on the World of Technology

"I hear there're rumors on the… uh… 'Internets.'"

"And one of the things I've used on the Google is to pull up maps."

"The Internet is not something you just dump something on. It's not a big truck. It's a series of tubes."

> — Sen. Ted Stevens (R-AK) speaking to the Senate as chairman of the Commerce, Science and Transportation committee in June 2006

"Every one of us sitting here tonight have our lives dramatically improved because we have a space program, whether it's these screens that we see here or the incredible electronics that we use…. Now, whether we need to send someone to Mars I don't know. But I tell you what, if we do, I have a few suggestions and maybe Hillary could be on the first rocket to Mars."

> — former Arkansas governor Mike Huckabee at a November 2007 Republican debate, referring to Democratic candidate Sen. Clinton

"The Internet is a great way to get on the Net."

> — Sen. Bob Dole as a presidential candidate

POLITICIANS
ON DRUGS

"When I was in England, I experimented with marijuana a time or two and I didn't like it. I didn't inhale."

— Bill Clinton in 1992, as a Democratic hopeful for president

When asked if he had ever smoked pot: "You bet I did. And I enjoyed it."

— Michael Bloomberg, New York City mayor, in 2002

"I didn't just experiment with marijuana, if you know what I mean."

— former Clinton strategist James Carville explaining why he would never run for governor of Louisiana in a speech at Tulane University on April 19, 2007

Hey, Don't Bogart That Pill!

About medicinal marijuana: "I'm not one that generally favors increasing the number of drugs that people have, particularly if there's a chance for abuse. Now, if a doctor prescribes, and it is in a form like a pill or some type of form that is not so much a recreational endeavor, I think that is a different discussion."

— former Arkansas governor Mike Huckabee in November 2007, answering a question by video on 10questions.com

TESTIMONY:
DANCING WITH WORDS

Washington movers and shakers can be masters of careful word choice. One of the best times to watch the verbal two-step is when these high-profile figures are under oath.

"It depends on what the meaning of the word 'is' is."
— President Bill Clinton, testifying before the Grand Jury in August 1998 about whether he had previously lied under oath

Maybe You Should Look Into Those Memory Pills

In April 2007, attorney general Alberto Gonzales earned a reputation for poor memory when he testified at a Senate hearing into the firings of eight U.S. federal prosecutors. The Senate Judiciary Committee hearing was called because of allegations that the dismissals had been politically motivated. Gonzales faced criticism for his testimony; while under oath, he said, on 71 different occasions, that he could not recall details relating to the firings.

FLASHBACK

"I was provided with additional input that was radically different from the truth. I assisted in furthering that version."
— Lt. Col. Oliver North, testifying at the Iran-Contra trials in 1987

JOKES GONE BAD

Politicians are professional public speakers and often try to warm up their audiences with jokes. Sometimes their humorous attempts garner laughs; other times, they end up suffering from foot-in-mouth disease.

Housewife Elaine Johnson, who lost a son in Iraq, recalls George W. Bush's comments when he gave her and five other bereaved women a presidential coin to commemorate their sons' deaths: "He gave six of us a presidential coin, [told] us not to tell the rest of the people that was there, and then, after that, he told us, 'Don't go sell it on eBay.'"

At a fund-raising event in 2004, Hillary Clinton introduced a quote by Gandhi by saying, "He ran a gas station down in St. Louis… No, Mahatma Gandhi was a great leader of the 20th century."

"Those weapons of mass destruction have got to be somewhere!"
— President George W. Bush in a video played at the 2004 White House Correspondents' Dinner. The video showed Bush searching under furniture in the White House Oval Office for the elusive weapons while making this comment.

MORE MANGLED, MUDDLED AND
MIXED-UP WORDS

"Families is where our nation finds home, where wings
take dream."

> — George W. Bush, campaigning in Wisconsin in October 2000

"The president can claim executive privilege. But in this case, I
think with a lifetime appointment to the Supreme Court, you can't
play, you know, hide the salami, or whatever it's called."

> — Howard Dean in October 2005 as chairman of the DNC, commenting
> on the lack of public information about Harriet Miers, a nominee to
> the Supreme Court, on *Hardball with Chris Matthews*

"Our enemies are innovative and resourceful—and so are we.
They never stop thinking about new ways to harm our country
and our people—and neither do we."

> — President George W. Bush in August 2004, at a ceremony where he
> signed a bill to increase defense funding

He Probably Didn't Mean that Second One...

"I hope I stand for anti-bigotry, anti-Semitism, anti-racism."

> — Vice President George H.W. Bush, while campaigning in 1988

Just a Slip of the Tongue

"As I was telling my hus— as I was telling President Bush…"

— Condoleezza Rice in 2004, as George W. Bush's wife—uh, national security advisor

It Can When It Moves from Place to Place…

"A zebra cannot change its spots."

— Sen. Al Gore (D-TN) in 1992 about George H.W. Bush, while campaigning for the vice presidency

Must Be One of Those Little-Known Diseases…

"We haven't had any attacks as of anybody receiving West Nile virus or encephalopoulus."

— Tommy Thompson at a state fair in 2002. Thompson (R), a former governor of Wisconsin and a one-time 2008 presidential hopeful, was the secretary of health and human services when he made this remark. Presumably, he meant "encephalitis."

Someone Needs a Dictionary

"Republicans understand the importance of bondage between a mother and child."

— Sen. Dan Quayle, while campaigning for the 1988 election

"We have got to eliminate in the future any red tape that helps families."

> — Bill Richardson, governor of New Mexico and 2008 Democratic presidential hopeful, commenting on the government's response to Hurricane Katrina in a July 2007 debate. He quickly corrected himself to "that helps the devastation."

So *That's* What They Mean by Presence of Mind...

"This is still the greatest country in the world, if we just will steel our wills and lose our minds."

> — Bill Clinton as governor of Arkansas, speaking at the University of Hawaii in 1992. (He intended to say "use our minds.")

"What a waste it is to lose one's mind. Or not to have a mind. How true that is."

> — Dan Quayle at a fundraiser for the United Negro College Fund in 1989. He was trying to say "a mind is a terrible thing to waste."

Washington Was More Creative Than We Had Thought...

"President Washington, President Lincoln, President Wilson and President Roosevelt have all authorized electronic surveillance on a far broader scale."

> — U.S. attorney general Alberto Gonzales in February 2006, speaking to the U.S. Senate Judiciary Committee about the National Security Agency's authority for surveillance

Chapter Seven

OVAL OFFICE

THE WHITE HOUSE:
IT AIN'T ALL IT'S CRACKED UP TO BE

We may imagine that life on Pennsylvania Avenue is full of glamour and excitement because it's the center for the political movers and shakers of the world's strongest nation. However, as these veterans tell us, life at the White House is not all power and prestige.

Run, George, Run!

"I try to go for longer runs, but it's tough around here at the White House on the outdoor track. It's sad that I can't run longer. It's one of the saddest things about the presidency."

> — George W. Bush in an interview with *Runner's World*, quoted in *The Washington Post* on Aug. 21, 2002

"Except for the occasional heart attack, I never felt better."

> — Vice President Dick Cheney in June 2003

About his plans after retiring as press secretary: "I want to do something more relaxing—like dismantle live nuclear weapons."

> — then-press secretary Ari Fleischer in May 2003, when announcing he would be leaving his position at the White House

The Most Powerful Man in the World

"I think I may need a bathroom break? Is this possible?"

> — President George W. Bush in a note to Secretary of State Condoleezza Rice during a UN meeting in September 2005. The note was captured in a photograph by Reuters.

"Being president is like running a cemetery: you've got a lot of people under you and nobody's listening."

> — President Bill Clinton in 1995, in a speech in Galesburg, Illinois

"I've worked for four presidents and watched two others up close, and I know that there's no such thing as a routine day in the Oval Office."

> — Vice President Dick Cheney in October 2004

"People ask me why I left Washington; I said I longed for the realism and sincerity of Hollywood."

> — former senator and 2008 presidential hopeful Fred Thompson in May 2007, at a Republican fundraising dinner

FLASHBACK

"As to the presidency, the two happiest days of my life were those of my entrance upon the office and my surrender of it."

— Martin Van Buren, 8th U.S. president

THE POWER
OF THE PRESIDENT

The office of the president, of course, is not without its charms.

"More and more, I wish that I had the opportunity to do the things that only a president can do."

> — former Tennessee senator Fred Thompson in June 2007, to Sean Hannity on *Hannity and Colmes.*

George Bush Sr. disliked broccoli to the extent that, in 1990, he banned the green veggie from the presidential plane, Air Force One, and the tables at the White House.

"The president has kept all the promises he intended to keep."

> — George Stephanopolous, as an aide to Bill Clinton, in a 1996 interview with Larry King

---

FLASHBACK

"Well, when the president does it, that means that it is not illegal."

— Richard Nixon, explaining his interpretation of executive privilege in a televised interview with David Frost in May 1977

THE REINS OF
POWER

These politicians feel strongly that the reins of power should be held pretty tightly.

"When you have an efficient government, you have a dictatorship."
— Harry S. Truman, 33rd U.S. president

"If this were a dictatorship, it'd be a heck of a lot easier, just so long as I'm the dictator."
— George W. Bush, on Dec. 18, 2000, just after the Supreme Court announced its decision that settled the 2000 election and made him president

"Freedom is about authority. Freedom is about the willingness of every single human being to cede to lawful authority a great deal of discretion about what you do."
— Rudolph Giuliani as New York City mayor in 1994, on how to reduce crime

"You know the problem with diplomacy: it takes a long time to get something done. If you're acting alone, you can move more quickly."
— President George W. Bush at a Chicago press conference in July 2006

THE WHITE HOUSE AND
THE MEDIA

"I don't watch the nightly newscasts on TV, nor do I watch the endless hours of people giving their opinion about things. I don't read the editorial pages; I don't read the columnists. It can be a frustrating experience to pay attention to somebody's false opinion."

> — George W. Bush, quoted in Bill Sammon's *Misunderestimated: The President Battles Terrorism, John Kerry, and the Bush Haters* (2004). Sammon was then senior White House correspondent for *The Washington Times*.

"There are still places where people think the function of the media is to provide information."

> — Dan Rottenberg, White House spokesperson, quoted in *The Patriot Ledger* in February 2000

FLASHBACK

About the media: "In the United States today, we have more than our share of nattering nabobs of negativism. They have formed their own 4-H club—the hopeless, hysterical hypochondriacs of history."

— Vice President Spiro Agnew in a speech to a Republican convention in California in September 1970

DICK CHENEY

Maybe I Should Practice My Cackle...

"What's wrong with my image? Am I the evil genius in the corner that nobody ever sees come out of his hole? It's a nice way to operate, actually."

— Dick Cheney in a January 2004 interview

"I'm not going to get into a name-calling match with someone who had a nine percent approval rating."

— Sen. Harry Reid (D-NV), Senate majority leader, at a April 24, 2007 press conference, refusing to respond to criticism from Vice President Dick Cheney that the Democrats calling the Iraq War "lost" was nothing more than "defeatism"

"Vice President Cheney came up to see the Republicans yesterday. You can always tell when the Republicans are restless because the vice president's motorcade pulls into the Capitol and Darth Vader emerges...."

— Democratic presidential candidate Sen. Hillary Clinton at a September 2007 fundraiser

GEORGE
DUBYA

Part of George W. Bush's legacy will be his fearless approach to the English language.

The "-Ers" of Bush

"Suiciders are willing to kill innocent life in order to send the projection that this is an impossible mission."

— on April 3, 2007

"That's why we are inconveniencing air traffickers, to make sure nobody is carrying weapons on airplanes."

— on April 3, 2007

"I'm the decider and I decide what's best. And what's best is for Don Rumsfeld to remain."

— on April 18, 2006. In December 2006, Rumsfeld left his post as defense secretary.

"As you know, my position is clear—I'm the commander guy."

— on May 2, 2007

"If you are a single mother with two children, which is the toughest job in America as far as I'm concerned, and you're working hard to put food on your family."

— in January 2000

"America needs a military where our breast and brightest are proud to serve."

> — to the troops at Fort Stewart, Georgia, on Feb. 12, 2001

President Bush spoke to the FBI Academy in Virginia in 2003. Government intelligence gathering had greatly improved, he told the audience. While raising his right hand, he said, "The left hand now knows what the right hand," at which point he raised his left hand, "is doing." This beautiful TV moment became part of David Letterman's Top 10 George Bush Moments, which he presented via satellite at the 2007 White House Correspondents' Dinner.

"It's an old saying in Texas, I believe also in Tennessee. Fool me once... shame on you. Fool me... Can't get fooled again."

> — to a Nashville, Tennessee audience, on Sept. 17, 2002. This is the Bush version of: "Fool me once, shame on you. Fool me twice, shame on me."

Most Ironic Requirement Ever

"What the president has said all along is that he wants to make sure that people who become American citizens have a command of the English language."

> — White House press secretary Tony Snow on May 19, 2006

THE ACORN
DOESN'T FALL FAR FROM THE TREE

We love to make fun of George W. for his creative phrasing, but it seems that he comes by it honestly. As Ann Richards, former governor of Texas, said about Bush Sr., "Poor George. He can't help it. He was born with a silver foot in his mouth." Here are some quotes by the first President Bush.

"Fluency in English is something that I'm often not accused of."
— in 1989

"Please just don't look at part of the glass, the part that is only less than half full."
— at a news conference in November 1991

"I just am not one who—who flamboyantly believes in throwing a lot of words around."
— in 1990

"Your snorkel will fill up and there will be no justice."
— in September 1991, about the need to manage the sea of presidential paperwork

Chapter Eight

TOE THE PARTY LINE

ASSES
AND ELEPHANTS

America's two-party system is one of the things that distinguishes it from many other countries around the world.

About the Democrats and the Republicans: "The two parties have spoiled our country. They're the real spoilers."
 — **Ralph Nader in February 2008 when announcing his plans to run as an independent in the 2008 presidential election**

"Republicans believe every day is the 4th of July, but Democrats believe every day is April 15."
 — **President Ronald Reagan, quoted in the New York Times in 1984**

"As people do better, they start voting like Republicans—unless they have too much education and vote Democratic, which proves there can be too much of a good thing."
 — **Karl Rove, quoted in the February 2001 issue of The New Yorker. Rove was then senior advisor to the president.**

"The Democrats said, 'We don't know what's wrong with America, but we can fix it.' The Republicans said, 'There's nothing wrong with America, and we can fix that.'"
 — **P.J. O'Rourke in his 2003 book Parliament of Whores**

AGAINST
DEMOCRATS

In 2004, Conservative pundit Rush Limbaugh spoke out strongly against Sen. John Kerry's policy and track record. On a more personal level, he noted, "He is Howard Dean without the charisma." Continuing on the same theme, he also said, "He gets out of a coffin every day to go to work."

Former senator Bob Dole, a man with a reputation for being a bit stiff himself, noted in 2000, "When Al Gore gives a fireside chat, the fire goes out."

About Nancy Pelosi, the newly elected Speaker of the House: "It's like listening to a cross between a Stepford wife and Jesse Jackson."

— *The Economist*, Nov. 2, 2006

FLASHBACK

"A liberal is a man with both feet planted firmly in the air."

— **Adlai Stevenson, former governor of Illinois and U.S. ambassador to the UN**

AGAINST
REPUBLICANS

When Sen. Tim Johnson (D-SD) had a stroke shortly after the Democrats had won a 51-seat Senate majority, Joy Behar blamed the White House. This exchange between Behar and *The View* co-host Elisabeth Hasselbeck is from December 2006.

BEHAR: "Is there such a thing as a man-made stroke? In other words, did someone do this to him?"

HASSELBECK: "Why is everything coming from the liberal perspective a conspiracy?"

BEHAR: "I know what this [Republican] party is capable of."

"I hate the Republicans and everything they stand for, but I admire their discipline and their organization."

— Howard Dean in January 2005, to the Association of Democratic State Chairs at a meeting in New York City

About Giuliani: "There's only three things he mentions in a sentence: a noun, and a verb and 9/11."

— Sen. Joe. Biden (D-DE) at a Democratic candidates' debate in November 2007. He also said Giuliani was "the most under-qualified man since George W. Bush to seek the presidency."

AGAINST
GEORGE W. BUSH

The sitting president is always a target for critics, and George Bush Jr. is no exception.

In his 2004 book *The Price of Loyalty*, former treasury secretary Paul O'Neill describes George W. Bush's behavior during cabinet meetings as "a blind man in a room of deaf people."

"How can 59,054,087 people be so DUMB?"

— headline in the British tabloid *The Daily Mirror* on Nov. 4, 2004, the day after George W. Bush's re-election

"Did the training wheels fall off?"

— Sen. John Kerry in May 2004, after hearing that President Bush fell off a bicycle he was riding.

FLASHBACK

About George Bush Sr.: "If ignorance goes to forty dollars a barrel, I want drilling rights to George Bush's head."

— Jim Hightower, political activist and former Texas commissioner of agriculture

"The president was so excited about Tom Friedman's book, *The World is Flat*. As soon as he saw the title, he said, 'You see? I was right.'"

— Sen. Barack Obama at the Gridiron Club's 2006 dinner

Dennis Kucinich visited *The Colbert Report* in October 2007. At one point in the interview, host Stephen Colbert noted that the Cleveland congressman carries a copy of the U.S. Constitution and Declaration of Independence. Holding up the pocket-size volume, Colbert asked Kucinich if he had shrunk down the document himself. Kucinich replied, "No, no. George Bush already did that."

About the president's priorities when reading the newspaper: "Sometimes the comics, but, you know, he was really into the sports pages."

— former White House chief of staff Andrew Card in 2006

"I sometimes feel that Alfred E. Neuman is in charge in Washington."

— Sen. Hillary Clinton, speaking at the Aspen Institute's Ideas Festival in Colorado in July 2005

Chapter Nine

THE WILD
AND
THE WACKY

COLBERT
FOR PRESIDENT

Mark Twain once said, "Irreverence is the champion of liberty and its only sure defense." Thanks to comedians like Stephen Colbert, liberty is alive and well in presidential campaigns.

In mid-October 2007, in his best satiric fashion, Stephen Colbert of *The Colbert Report* announced plans to run for president. A week into Colbert's campaign, a national Rasmussen Report phone survey found that, in a match up against Hillary Clinton and Rudy Giuliani, 13 % of those surveyed chose Stephen Colbert. In another poll conducted by Republican polling firm Opinion Polling Strategies, Colbert garnered 2.3 % of the vote, placing ahead of serious candidates Bill Richardson (2.1 %), Dennis Kucinich (2.1 %) and Mike Gravel (less than 1 %).

Colbert didn't file as a Republican, and his Democratic campaign ended two weeks after it began when he was turned down by the South Carolina Democratic Counsel. Colbert reacted to the news with disappointment. He told his studio audience that he had prepared an impeachment speech for when he overstepped his presidential authority and that now he would never have the chance to use it.

More Pseudo-Politicians

Stephen Colbert was not the first comedian to mock the political process. Here are a few great lines from other humorists.

"A platform is something a candidate stands for and the voters fall for."

> — comedian Gracie Allen. Allen, George Burns' wife and comedy partner, ran for president in 1940. When she was asked her party affiliation, she replied, "I may take a drink now and then, but I never get affiliated."

"The difference between death and taxes is death doesn't get worse every time Congress meets."

> — humorist Will Rogers. He ran in 1928 for the Anti-Bunk Party. Rogers made the election promise, "If elected, I will resign."

"These lawmakers don't like to take graft and big bribes...but how else can they get the money to buy votes?"

> — satirist Pat Paulsen in a 1968 column about congressional ethics. When he ran for president in 1968, one of his campaign slogans was, "I've upped my standards. Now, up yours."

SPACED OUT!

Beware the Vulcan Mind-meld

"This president has listened to some people, the so-called Vulcans in the White House, the ideologues. But you know, unlike the Vulcans of *Star Trek* who made the decisions based on logic and fact, these guys make it on ideology. These aren't Vulcans. There are Klingons in the White House. But unlike the real Klingons of *Star Trek,* these Klingons have never fought a battle of their own. Don't let faux Klingons send real Americans to war."

> — Rep. David Wu (D-OR, 1999–) in a Jan. 10, 2007 speech on the floor of the House of Representatives

"Not a penny of public money has been or will be spent on Klingon translation."

> — Diane Linn, chair of the board of commissioners for Multnomah County, Oregon (2003–07) in a May 2003 press release. She issued the statement in response to her county approving translation of Klingon if mental patients require it.

Okay... But Who's Got the Ring?

"As the hobbits are going up Mount Doom, the Eye of Mordor is being drawn somewhere else. It's being drawn to Iraq and it's not being drawn to the U.S. You know what? I want to keep it on Iraq. I don't want the Eye to come back here to the United States."

> — Sen. Rick Santorum (R-PA, 1995–2007) in October 2006, on why it was wise to remain in Iraq

To the Cosmos and Beyond...

Rep. Dennis Kucinich (D-OH, 1997–), 2008 presidential hopeful, often casts his eyes to the heavens. For example, he's introduced four versions of a Space Preservation Act intended to prevent the militarization of space. Here are some quotes that give us a glimpse into his expansive mind:

"The energy of the stars becomes us. We become the energy of the stars. Stardust and spirit unite and we begin: one with the universe, whole and holy. From one source, endless creative energy, bursting forth, kinetic, elemental; we, the earth, air, water and fire-source of nearly fifteen billion years of cosmic spiraling. We receive the blessings of the Eternal and we are showered with abundance. We ask and we receive. A universe of plenty flows to us, through us. It is in us. We become filled with endless possibilities."

— in a speech at the Praxis Peace Institute Conference in Croatia on June 9, 2002

"We're asking our country's leaders to take a holistic view of the world and to allow the globe, the sphere of the Earth herself, to exist free from an assault from space. All the universe should understand that we truly come in peace because we exist in peace."

— in a speech in Malibu, California on Feb. 23, 2002

BEAM ME UP

James Traficant, flamboyant congressman for Ohio (1985–2002), was known for his colorful one-minute speeches on the House floor.

"Madam Speaker, I agree with New York Mayor Giuliani for cutting funds to the Brooklyn Museum of Art. Their latest show features the bust of a man frozen in his own blood, a small pig sliced in half and preserved in a bottle of formaldehyde, and a portrait of the Virgin Mary splattered with elephant feces. Art, Madam Speaker? My ascot.

"Let us tell it like it is. The truth is the art world has gone from Michelangelo's Sistine Chapel to Lorena Bobbitt's pristine scalpel. Beam me up. I yield back the trash, not treasures, of the Brooklyn Museum of Disgusting Art."

— in a speech to the House of Representatives, Sept. 27, 1999

"Mr. Speaker, something does not add up. The number of accidental deaths involving guns average 1,500 per year; and the number of accidental deaths caused by doctors, surgeons, and hospitals average 120,000 a year—120,000 per year! That means the ratio of accidental medical-related deaths to accidental gun deaths is 80 to 1, 80 times more possible of being killed accidentally by a doctor than a gun. Tell me, Mr. Speaker, should we mandate a 5-day waiting period on vasectomies?"

— in a speech to the House of Representatives, April 4, 2000

"From the womb to the tomb, Madam Speaker, the Internal Rectal Service is one big enema. Think about it: they tax our income, they tax our savings, they tax our sex, they tax our property sales profits, they even tax our income when we die. Is it any wonder America is taxed off? We happen to be suffering from a disease called Taxes Mortis Americanus. Beam me up. It is time to pass a flat, simple 15 percent sales tax, and fire these nincompoops at the IRS. Think about it."

— in a speech to the House of Representatives, March 20, 2001

In 2002, Traficant was accused of bribery, racketeering and tax evasion. He chose to represent himself against the charges. He was ultimately convicted on 10 felony charges.

"I want you to disregard all the opposing counsel has said. I think they're delusionary. I think they've had something funny for lunch in their meal. I think they should be handcuffed to a chain-link fence, flogged, and all of their hearsay evidence should be thrown the hell out. And if they lie again, I'm going to go over there and kick them in the crotch. Thank you very much."

— in a statement to the House ethics subcommittee during his 2002 hearing

"If you don't get those cameras out of my face, I'm gonna go 8.6 on the Richter scale with gastric emissions that'll clear this room!"

— to journalists covering his hearing

QUITE AN
HONOR

During an April 2005 naming ceremony, researcher Quentin Wheeler heaped praise on the Bush administration, singling out President George W. Bush, Vice President Dick Cheney and Secretary Donald Rumsfeld.

Wheeler said, "We admire these leaders as fellow citizens who have the courage of their convictions and are willing to do the very difficult and unpopular work of living up to principles of freedom and democracy rather than accepting the expedient or popular." What did Wheeler name in honor of these politicians? Slime-eating bugs.

Wheeler, now head entomologist at the Natural History Museum in London, England, and a colleague, Kelly Miller, honored Bush, Cheney and Rumsfeld by naming three new species of Agathidium, or slime-mold beetles, after them. Wheeler and Miller are former Cornell University entomologists who were naming a total of 65 new species of slime-mold beetles.

The species named for the Republicans are *A. bushi*, *A. cheneyi* and *A. rumsfeldi*.

IT'S A
DOG'S LIFE

President Harry Truman was fond of saying, "If you need a friend in Washington, get yourself a dog." Here are some thoughts about four-legged friends.

"You may have read that the pups are sleeping on *The Washington Post* and the *New York Times*. It's the first time in history these papers have been used to prevent leaks."

— President George H.W. Bush in a May 1989 speech in Kentucky

On the Iraq War: "I will not withdraw even if Laura and Barney are the only ones supporting me."

— President George W. Bush, quoted by Bob Woodward in 2006. Bush was referring to his wife, Laura, and his Scottish terrier, Barney.

"My dog Millie knows more about foreign policy than these two bozos."

— President George H.W. Bush during the 1992 presidential campaign, about Bill Clinton and Al Gore

A
FINAL
THOUGHT

"The President must be greater than anyone else, but not better than anyone else. We subject him and his family to close and constant scrutiny and denounce them for things that we ourselves do every day. A Presidential slip of the tongue, a slight error in judgment—social, political, or ethical—can raise a storm of protest. We give the President more work than a man can do, more responsibility than a man should take, more pressure than a man can bear. We abuse him often and rarely praise him. We wear him out, use him up, eat him up. And with all this, Americans have a love for the President that goes beyond loyalty or party nationality; he is ours, and we exercise the right to destroy him."

— John Steinbeck in *America and Americans* (1966)

Index of Speakers

Quote *Slide* ™

Enjoy the newest form of puzzle fun: QuoteSlides, created by Peter Nesbitt of Don't Quote Me. To solve them, place letters into the grid to reveal a hidden political quote.

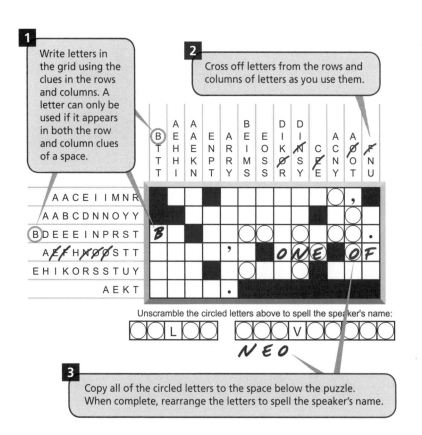

1 Write letters in the grid using the clues in the rows and columns. A letter can only be used if it appears in both the row and column clues of a space.

2 Cross off letters from the rows and columns of letters as you use them.

Unscramble the circled letters above to spell the speaker's name:

3 Copy all of the circled letters to the space below the puzzle. When complete, rearrange the letters to spell the speaker's name.

For more puzzle and game fun, visit www.dontquoteme.com.

QuoteSlide™ 1

This politician served as U.S. ambassador to the UN from 1961 to 1965. He is famous for a confrontation with Soviet ambassador Valerian Zorin during the Cuban Missile Crisis.

TIP

Look for columns that have only one or two different letters. Checking those letters in the corresponding rows will often allow you to place letters.

AACEIIMNR

AABCDNNOYY

BDEEEINPRST

AEFHNOOSTT

EHIKORSSTUY

AEKT

Unscramble the circled letters above to spell the speaker's name:

QuoteSlide™ 2

This politician was a five-time senator from Arizona. He ran for president in 1964, losing to Lyndon B. Johnson. He was also an avid amateur photographer who became known for his Western landscapes.

TIP

Look for any letters that appear only once in the puzzle.

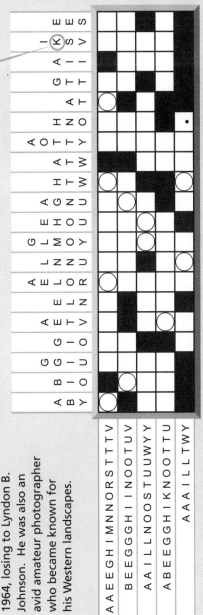

Unscramble the circled letters above to spell the speaker's name:

| A A E E G H I M N N O R S T T T V |
| B E E G G G H I I N O O T U V |
| A A I L L N O O S T U U W Y Y |
| A B E E G G H I K N O O T T U |
| A A A I L L T W Y |

QuoteSlide™ 3

This journalist and essayist was awarded a special Pulitzer Prize in 1978 for his body of work. Today, he's remembered for his children's books.

ACCDEEHIMORSTY

CCEEIINNOPRRSSTUU

AAAEFHHHLMNORTT

AEEEEFHLOOPPRT

AEGHHIMNORTT

AEEFFHHILMOTT

Unscramble the circled letters above to spell the speaker's name:

○ . B .   W ○ ○ ○ ○

QuoteSlide™ 4

This U.S. author is known in the billiards world for his *Standard Book of Pool and Billiards*, first published in 1978, but has also written seven novels and compiled several volumes of quotations.

Unscramble the circled letters above to spell the speaker's name:

○	○	○	B		○	○	
○	B	○	○	○		○	

A G G I I M N N O O P R S U Y
A D G H L M N O O S U
C I I L N O O O P S S T T
A A C E G H H N N O O T T
E F G H I I M N O O P R R S T
E E F F H I I L O R S S T

QuoteSlide™ 5

This essayist, literary critic and satirist wrote nearly 3,000 newspaper columns. His works often criticized public officials, religion and democracy.

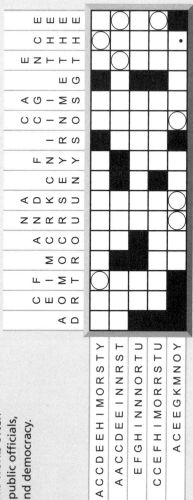

ACCDEEHIMORSTY

AACCDEEINNRST

EFGHINNORTU

CCEFHIMORRSTU

ACEEGKMNOY

Unscramble the circled letters above to spell the speaker's name:

QuoteSlide™ 6

This American writer spent years traveling the world. He wrote about some of those experiences in his book *Following the Equator* (1897).

E E E O O P P R S S U U W Y							
A A D D I I N N O T							
E E E O O P P R S S U U W Y							
A B E E F M M O R							
B C E G I N O R S S T U							
A E E E F L M P R S T Y							

Unscramble the circled letters above to spell the speaker's name:

QuoteSlide™ 7

This Soviet leader is remembered for passionately denouncing his predecessor, Joseph Stalin, and the effects of Stalin's control over the Soviet Union.

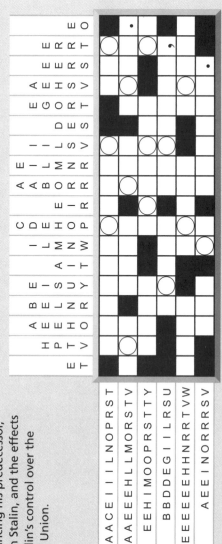

Unscramble the circled letters above to spell the speaker's name:

```
A A C E I I I L N O P R S T
A A E E E E H L L M O R S T V
E E H I M O O P R S T T Y
B B D D E G I I L R S U
E E E E E E H H N R R T V W
A E E I N O R R R S V
```

QuoteSlide™ 8

This statesman served as the first chancellor of the German Empire and was a key figure in the 1871 unification of Germany.

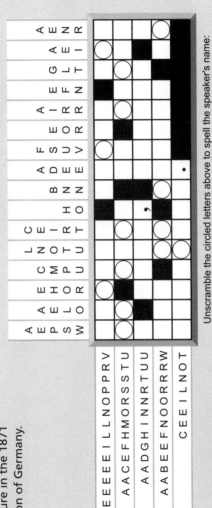

Unscramble the circled letters above to spell the speaker's name:

○○○○○ ○○○ ○○○○○○○○ K

EEEEEILLNOPPRV
AACEFHMORSSTU
AADGHINNRTUU
AABEEFNOORRRW
CEEILNOT

QuoteSlide™ 9

This political satirist has written for *National Lampoon, The Atlantic Monthly* and *Rolling Stone*. Known for his sense of humor, he has authored 13 books.

Unscramble the circled letters above to spell the speaker's name:

G	I	E	E	A	A	A	D	A	A	E	E	A	E	E	S
L	K	K	E	N	A	E	D	G	G	G	C	B	E	I	T
M	O	N	I	S	I	N	E	G	P	H	H	M	K	N	Y
	T	O	Y	Y	T	Z	N	P	O	E	R	R	O	Y	
	Y	V	G	G	V	I	O	V	W	W	N	S	R		

EEGGGIIMNNNORTVV

ADEEIMNNOOPRSWY

ACEGGIIKLNRV

ADEEHIKKNSSWYY

AABEEEGNOOTTY

QuoteSlide™ 10

This American poet earned four Pulitzer Prizes for his work. One of his favorite themes was rural life in New England.

A A B E I I L L R S	
A A M N O O T	
A B D D D E I M N O R	
A E H I K O S T T	
D E I I N N O S W	
A A E L Q R R U	

Unscramble the circled letters above to spell the speaker's name:

F ◯◯◯◯   ◯◯◯◯◯◯

QuoteSlide™ 11

This charismatic woman worked in vaudeville and film before opening a speakeasy called The 400 Club during Prohibition.

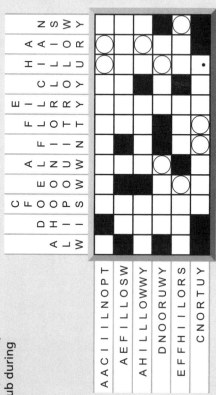

AACIILNOPT
AEFILLOSW
AHILLOWWY
DNOORUWY
EFFHIILORS
CNORTUY

Unscramble the circled letters above to spell the speaker's name:

QuoteSlide™ 12

The speaker of this quote got his start as a rider and trick roper for Texas Jack's Wild West Circus. In later life, he became a celebrated humorist, author and movie star.

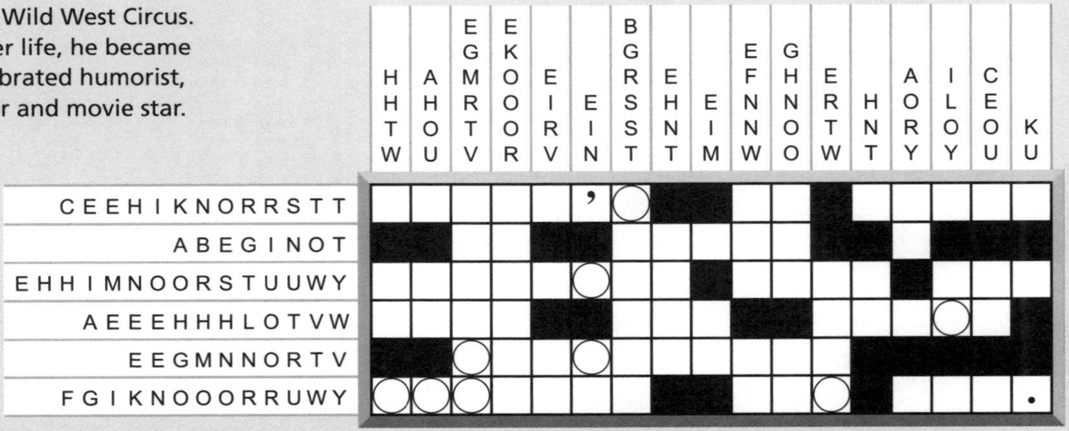

Grid letters (columns):

H A E E B E E H A I C
H H G M G G F R O L E
T O R O R E H N H R O
O T O O E S E N T O O
W U V R S T N N W T Y
. . . . T N I M . Y U
. . . . . T W O T U U
K

Word banks:
- C E E H I K N O R R S T T
- A B E G I N O T
- E H H I M N O O R S T U U W Y
- A E E E H H H L O T V W
- E E G M N N O R T V
- F G I K N O O O R R U W Y

Unscramble the circled letters above to spell the speaker's name:

◯ ◯ L ◯ ◯ ◯ ◯ ◯ ◯

QuoteSlide™ 13

This American author based one of his most famous works, *Slaughterhouse-Five*, on his experiences as a prisoner of war in Dresden, Germany.

Unscramble the circled letters above to spell the speaker's name:

EEIOORRRSTTTU

AEEGIKMNNNOOPRUW

AACDDEHINORSTTV

CGHHHILOOORSUY

ACGIILNNNRSSSU

CEHNORTTUY

QuoteSlide™ 14

This lawyer was a prominent defense attorney. One of his most famous cases was the 1925 Scopes Monkey Trial.

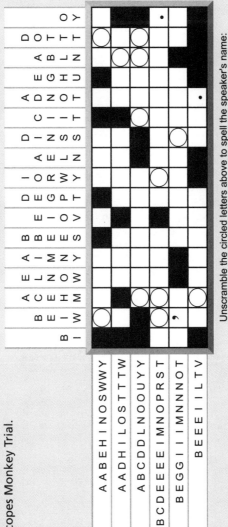

Unscramble the circled letters above to spell the speaker's name:

⬡⬡⬡⬡⬡⬡⬡⬡ R R ⬡

A A B E H I N O S W W Y

A A D H I L O S T T T W

A B C D D L N O O U Y Y

B C D E E E I M N O P R S T

B E G G I I M N N N O T

B E E E I I L T V

QuoteSlide™ Puzzle Answers

Puzzle #1
"In America, anybody can be president. That's one of the risks you take." — Adlai Stevenson

Puzzle #2
"A government that is big enough to give you all you want is big enough to take it all away." — Barry Goldwater

Puzzle #3
"Democracy is the recurrent suspicion that more than half of the people are right more than half of the time." — E.B. White

Puzzle #4
"A promising young man should go into politics so that he can go on promising for the rest of his life." — Robert Byrne

Puzzle #5
"Democracy is the art and science of running the circus from the monkey cage." — H.L. Mencken

Puzzle #6
"Suppose you were an idiot. And suppose you were a member of Congress. But I repeat myself." — Mark Twain

Puzzle #7
"Politicians are the same all over. They promise to build bridges, even where there are no rivers." — Nikita Khrushchev

Puzzle #8
"People never lie so much as after a hunt, during a war or before an election." — Otto von Bismarck

Puzzle #9
"Giving government money and power is like giving car keys and whiskey to a teenage boy." — P.J. O'Rourke

Puzzle #10
"A liberal is a man too broad-minded to take his own side in a quarrel." — Robert Frost

Puzzle #11
"A politician is a fellow who will lay down your life for his country." — Texas Guinan

Puzzle #12
"There's no trick to being a humorist when you have the whole government working for you." — Will Rogers

Puzzle #13
"True terror is to wake up one morning and discover that your high school class is running the country." — Kurt Vonnegut

Puzzle #14
"When I was a boy I was told that anybody could become president. I'm beginning to believe it." — Clarence Darrow